The
Gift of
Aging

**Navigating the Challenges
of Growing Old**

Donald Zoller

The Gift of Aging
Copyright © 2024 by Donald Zoller
ISBN: 979-8-35095-692-4

Cover Design by Liliana Zoller

Printed in the United States of America

A Dedication

For My Three Sons

Gregory, Graham, and Garth
Who will in the Autumn of Life
Pick up this Book
To understand what Aging
Is all about.

Unknown may be the path I tread,
Along its dusty road I am not alone,
Strewn with rocks and pits at every turn,
Yet secure!
With confidence I trust
In the One who is at my side,
Reminding me with words of love,
"I will never leave you or forsake you.
I will always be your Guide!"
From Isaiah 41:10-13

—Don Zoller, 2018

Finding Your Way Around

Contents

As it Was in Our Beginning

*F*or you created my inmost being;
you knit me together in my mother's womb.
I praise you because I am fearfully and wonderfully made;
your works are wonderful, I know that full well.
My frame was not hidden from you
when I was made in the secret place,
when I was woven together in the depths of the earth,
Your eyes saw my unformed body;
All the days ordained for me
were written in your book
before one of them came to be.
How precious to me are your thoughts, O God!
How vast is the sum of them!
Psalm 139:13–17
New International Version

Let's Start
Introduction

A Note from the Author

An introduction to any book should help the reader navigate the contents of the chapters with ease and comfort. The introduction should paint an inviting landscape where the reader can enjoy the journey while engaging in the book's narrative. It should also satisfy the curious, informing them of the book's contents, arrangement, and some of the thinking that went into its creation. If done well, an introduction will compel the reader irresistibly forward with excitement to discover and explore ways that may personally affect their lives. For some, reading the introduction can be a quick way to decide if the book is worth their effort to read. Now, let's see what *The Gift of Aging* has to say.

About The Book

We are aging. To state it bluntly, we are getting old! *The Gift of Aging* speaks plainly about the issues and challenges of aging, both the good and the not-so-good. Most importantly, this book focuses on God's plan and purpose for us as we age.

Just because we are old doesn't mean we are done with living. We're not relics displayed on the shelf only to be admired and occasionally dusted. No. With anticipation, *The Gift of Aging* helps us step into God's story for our lives with joy and thanksgiving and to seek His glory within the boundaries and challenges given to us.

The Table of Contents is the road map for specific challenges we encounter in the Autumn of Life. Yet, as we shall see, God is able to transform each challenge into a gift—a gift of aging.

Woven throughout the book are comments from seniors who have chosen to remain anonymous. These comments will help us see we're not alone in facing these challenges. As a senior member of this older and distinguished community, I have included my reflections and experiences. Also included are sources beyond my comments.

The book is written for those who are reasonably mobile and cognitively responsive. However, the book acknowledges the reality that some in this aging population have life-threatening or terminal illnesses. Thus, their mobility and cognition are limited. Their interaction with life is usually confined to clinical or family care. Topics related to these special needs and challenges are not included.

The Gift of Aging is written from a Christian perspective. However, it welcomes all who are interested in aging and seek to understand the challenges of growing old. Together, we will glean life principles of growing old and discover the gift of aging.

A little more white space between lines, a slightly larger font size, and no hyphenated words at the end of lines offer an easier reading experience for we who are older. Written in a casual style, the book captures the informality of conversation around the kitchen table.

Putting the Book in Perspective

The term "aging," used in this book, includes those in the *Autumn of Life*—mid-60s and beyond. Or whenever aging becomes a lifestyle problem.

Aging begins at birth. Growing older (and hopefully wiser) is predictable and expected. We pass quickly through the seasons of life, winding our way to the Autumn of Life. Only when excessive wrinkles and waning strength become a reality does aging become uncomfortably noticeable and, for many, concerning. The *Gift of Aging* will address these concerns.

Books and articles on aging are prolific. Bookshelves, the Internet, and social media are brimming with *"How-to"* help for older people. How to stay healthy by eating correctly, staying hydrated, exercising, and getting enough sleep. How to remain actively engaged with others, have positive mental health habits, be financially secure, and so the list goes on. Oh yes. How to live until you're 110 or older is always a winner.

But why is so much written about senior wellness? Perhaps one answer is many older adults don't try to achieve a healthier life. They may view such an effort as *"nice to do, but not for me."* They may decide it's *"too late in life"* to begin. *"Why bother?"*

A noticeable gap in the "how-to" tutorials is the spiritual dimension of an older person. Spiritual uncertainties and doubts may plague the minds of many older people. *The Gift of Aging* highlights these uncertainties and provides answers to end-of-life questions.

Living life differently with renewed purpose and attitude is never too late. Let's read on and discover what that renewed life might look like.

Final Thoughts About the Book

Life is finite. Death is inevitable:

Since his days are determined, and the number of his months is with you, and you have appointed his limits that he cannot pass. Job 14:5

However, *The Gift of Aging* focuses on our remaining time—however long it may be—to live that time in thanksgiving and joy before departing this life.

Yes, this is another book on aging, but hopefully, it will be a book with a difference. *The Gift of Aging* calls us to face this final phase of life realistically while avoiding cynicism, self-focus, despair, self-pity, or resignation. While we have breath, we are alive. Because we are alive, we as older adults still have value. We may think we have only a "spoonful" of limited usefulness. But if we are breathing, we have value and a purpose to live. Hopefully, *The Gift of Aging* will help you discover that purpose.

Living in the Autumn of Life can be difficult and filled with challenges that may seem overwhelming. Later in the book, we will meet Myrna and Jean. They will show us that remaining productive as an older person is possible no matter how difficult life may be. While navigating its challenges, God intends aging to be part of our human experience and enjoyed as a gift from Him.

Finally, *The Gift of Aging* seeks to launch sedentary seniors from their rocking chairs to live with purpose and joy. Deciding to leave the rocking chair behind, growing old can become a new adventure in living— living God's way and tasting what will soon be experienced in His presence, where aging, suffering, and death are no more. *Won't that be wonderful?*

The Word of God, the Bible, and the Holy Spirit guide us to navigate this critical phase of life. Thus, Scripture is sprinkled throughout the book to offer encouragement, hope, and an eternal perspective on aging.

Come! Let's discover how aging can be a true gift in our Autumn of Life.

They still bear fruit in old age; they are ever full of sap and green, to declare that the Lord is upright.
Psalm 92:14–15a

Accepting

Accepting a gift is usually an easy thing to do. We learn from childhood to say "Thank You" for every gift received. But, frankly, not all gifts are seen as useful or wanted. These usually find their place in an out-of-the-way drawer, saved for a "white elephant" gift, or returned to the store in exchange for something truly wanted. We all have experienced these challenging gifts in our lifetime.

Accepting getting old can be a challenge. Although many believe getting old is not a gift, in this Chapter, we will consider accepting aging as a gift from God. We will discover how to accept ourselves as we grow older and to thank Him for His gift. Overcoming the challenges of aging is the perfect gift for any occasion!

Accepting What Our Mirror Reveals

One day, not long ago, I passed by the mirror in my bathroom. There, looking back at me, was an old man—at least, he looked old. His sagging skin and wrinkles clearly defined his age. Staring briefly at one another, the old man in the mirror seemed to speak to me in an unflattering tone. "Don, you're old!"

That's rather rude, I thought. I didn't feel old, even at eighty-eight. Apart from the usual dents, scars, and minor pains of a well-worn life, I never considered myself old. But, upon closer reflection, I finally had to concede to what I saw in the mirror. *I am old!* Replacing my mirror wouldn't change that truth. Unless I had the witch's mirror from the story of Snow White, my mirror faithfully told me the truth about the image it reflected—me! As I really am!

The simple truth is this: the challenge of getting old is *accepting we are old*—yes, with sagging skin, wrinkles, and all the other features that come with aging. However, admitting we're old is the easy part. Embracing what we see in the mirror is sometimes more difficult. *How well are we handling that?*

God has given us a gift—His perfect gift of aging. This gift cannot be stashed in a drawer or returned to the store. And who wants an aging white elephant? Yet rarely do we say "Thank you" to the Giver for His gift.

We may not see aging as a gift. Pain, limitations, grief. Yes. *But not a gift!*

The mirror doesn't lie. It reflects the image of a person who continues to age each time we stand in front of it. Lingering at our mirror and thinking how we looked in past years can be depressing. For many, aging is a limitation. An interruption and, in fact, an annoyance. Plain and simple, it's hard to accept aging as a gift!

But how can aging be a gift when our body and mind say otherwise? When our mirror argues to the contrary?

* * * *

Yet with the restrictions aging brings, it doesn't mean adopting an inactive lifestyle. Convincing ourselves we no longer have purpose in life. In God's plan, if we have breath, we have a reason to live and to live fully within our limitations.

Let's not forget, our lives don't belong to us. They are only on loan from God, who created them! Every breath we take is a gift from Him. And every pain, grief, or sorrow can be His gift if we allow Him to bathe our tears and afflictions with His presence and love.

Aging is no surprise to God; neither is it unplanned. It has purpose. Aging is part of His redemptive plan to give us peace and joy in this final season of our journey.

Nevertheless, we all grow old. Unlike aged cheese, vintage wine, or even carefully wrapped fruit cake, our lives don't last, and, for most, they don't last well. And unlike cheese, wine, and fruit cake, the quality of life does not improve with time. There is *spoilage* and *decay.*

Physical and mental limitations increase. We can become socially irrelevant. Isolated! So much for aged cheese, vintage wine, and well-preserved fruit cake. *These we are not!*

Our aging preserves very little. Certainly not body or mind. But there is a way God uses aging as a gift. But first, let's look at a few things about aging we probably all struggle with.

Signs of Aging

People are becoming older and living longer. The older we get, the more of us there seem to be. But being like *them* is not always easy to accept. Someone recently said, "I disliked being around older people until I realized these are the same people that were in my high school graduation class."

Signs of aging usually begin toward the end of middle age (50+) and continue the older we become. A gradual loss of muscle strength and less-than-desirable skin tone are usually the first signs. Lifting heavy objects becomes more difficult. The ability to grip strongly and hang onto things firmly becomes a challenge. Hearing is more difficult, and prescriptions for eyeglasses change more frequently. Trips to the doctor are no longer occasional. As one senior said, "Going to the doctor becomes a form of weekly senior entertainment."

Although exercising, eating correctly, staying hydrated,[1] and getting adequate sleep promotes good health generally, these disciplines are essential for older adults. Older minds and bodies are deficit-challenged. A healthy life requires more attention to these essentials as we age. But these good habits do not *cure* signs of aging. They simply provide the life tools to keep mind and body a bit more fit and stronger for the journey ahead.

Aging may come with denials and excuses. Some may add extra layers of cosmetic paint or wrinkle-reducing lotions to hide what is evident in our unforgiving mirror. Others may feel the appropriate treatment is Botox. Unless medically prescribed, such a treatment can be a form of denial. Alas, a single treatment lasts only a few months.[2]

It is hard to ignore what the mirror reveals. Forty or fifty years ago, we may have admired the tone and shape of our reflection. However, the same body now stares at us with a different message. *You're old!*

Stepping away from the mirror, we may notice that our balance isn't what it used to be. We dare not dance, walk the high wire, or climb ladders—not even small ones. We don't walk as fast, either. Each step carefully measured. Uncertain, tenuous steps may feel like walking on marshmallows with the potential of an unexpected fall. And our frequent scrapes, blood spots, and bruises make us look like wounded warriors.

Then, there are the keys. And the other things we try to clutch in our hands. Our fingers seem coated with warm butter as these things slip freely from our hands onto the floor. There they lie. Daring us to pick them up. But the muscles in our back don't seem to bend in that direction as easily as they once did. *"Now, where did I put my grabber?"*

And what about those pesky packages that challenge our depleted strength? We all have shared the experience. The ones labeled "tear here" on easy-to-open packages. Sore fingers and broken fingernails result from struggling to free the vaulted contents. Finally, we may decide only scissors or pliers will do the job. Or, out of frustration, we return the package to the fridge to repeat the task another day, hoping something will change.

Here we are. We arrive in a room and don't remember why we're there. Forgetting what it was we came looking for. Oh, well. It probably wasn't all that important anyway. *Here's a tip: write a note about what you are looking for. Then, when you enter a room and wonder why you're there, refer to your note. That may help the forgetful mind. Hopefully, you remember where you put your note!*

Multitasking. When we were younger, we managed multiple activities with a magic wand. Accomplishing everything almost instantly. Like a circus ringmaster. Corralling children, cleaning house, answering the phone—seemingly all at the same time. According to one senior lady, "As we age, multitasking has a new meaning—*getting out of bed in the morning!*"

Most have little trouble going to bed. Yet, we may wonder what happened during the night that makes it physically harder to get up in the morning. Or we may question who put the glue on the chair, making it a challenge of strength and balance when we stand.

According to clinicians,[3] we become less flexible as we age. Our tendons get tighter around joints, and the cartilage between our joints deteriorates. There is also a general deterioration in ligaments, a reduction in fluid (synovial fluid) within the joints and tightening of muscles surrounding the joints. This condition is helped by repeated *sit-to-stand* exercises and drinking plenty of water. *For older adults, overcoming gravity is a constant challenge.*

These clues remind us that we are not as young or strong as we once were or would like to be. Accepting these inconveniences, frustrations, and annoyances as part of aging is seldom easy. Yes, growing old is difficult. Challenging.

* * * *

But as difficult as growing old may be, there is one who is constantly at our side to help and encourage. Jesus is ever present during our afflictions. Despair and self-pity quickly dissolve when we recognize He is there to help. He invites us to experience His strength in our weakness. As we learn to accept Him as our helper, we can more readily accept ourselves.

We look beyond our mirror to see Christ working His purpose through our lives anew. Accepting His perfect gift of love will overshadow all our mirror reveals into thanksgiving and joy—the gift of aging.

The Dark Side of the Mirror

The unforgiving mirror tells the truth about aging. Accepting and embracing what we see is the first step toward discovery and peace for our hearts and minds.

If we're not at peace with what we see in the mirror and deny what we really are, we will soon despair and become depressed. We may be tempted to gravitate toward our recliner and watch TV for most of our waking hours. Absorbing a distorted reality while incurring avoidable aches and pains that come with immobility.

Some may sit endlessly reflecting on the distant past, like someone waiting for a bus that never arrives. Spiraling downward, we can become cynical, angry, and difficult to be around. Our health will deteriorate. Life without purpose. Without initiative to embrace a productive lifestyle. Avoidable illnesses and emotional problems may soon follow. All this is the dark side of the mirror. But sadly, there is more.

Being overwhelmed by the realities of aging can lead to severe despair and self-inflicted death—suicide. Self-inflicted death among older people is not uncommon. Often resulting from a deep sense of loneliness, unforgiving guilt from the past, painful chronic illness, financial stress, or unreconciled grief from the loss of a loved one. Alcoholism and prescription drug overdose are the common means used for "quiet suicide."[4]

Feeling overwhelmed by adversities of aging, suicide becomes a reasonable alternative. "Life is too hard. I can't go on!" are usually their final words. Sadly, without hope or direction, suicide is often the only option for a self-focused life without God.

The Apostle Peter faced certain death as he kept his focus on overwhelming circumstances. He was drowning. Before being swallowed by the sea, he saw Jesus. With outstretched hand, the Lord extended His love toward Peter. In desperation, Peter grabbed onto Jesus. He was rescued. He was delivered. There is help! There is hope for the desperate! *(Matthew 14:28-33*

Accepting Change

Accepting the changing world around us can be a challenge to older people. Ceaseless change seems to invade our well-ordered lives. The pressure of change often disturbs what is comfortable and secure. We like our life the way it is. *If it ain't broken, it doesn't need fix'n!*

Change intrudes into all aspects of life. How we behave and interact with people, do business, turn on our TVs, or using our computers all demand that we change to fit in. Unsettling and annoying, we resist change as an intruder and disrupter of our lives as we would like them to be—*as it used to be!*

However, learning to accept change is essential for growing old gracefully and with gratitude. Chapter 4 (page 79) discusses the challenge of change in more detail.

From a Challenge to a Gift

Let's see how God takes the challenge of aging and transforms it into a gift—a gift especially designed by Him.

We begin by thanking God for the challenges of aging. A thankful attitude helps strengthen our faith-walk and causes us to increasingly become more dependent on His strength.

"Finally, be strong in the Lord and in the power of His strength." Ephesians 6:10

I take my first uncertain step of the day with a prayer: Not *"I need Thee every hour,"* but Lord, at my age, I need You moment by moment. You are my strength for each step I take! Thank you. *(Psalm 18:1–3)*

The Psalmist recognizes our human weakness while providing the answer: *My flesh and heart may fail, but God is the strength of my heart and my portion forever (Psalm 73:26).*

Trusting Him is where He wants us. Whether we are on the floor after a fall or struggling to open a package. Whatever our situation, a thankful response to God *during* our struggles is critical for overcoming the challenge of accepting whatever may come our way.

So we do not lose heart. Though our outer self is wasting away, our inner self is being renewed day by day. For this light momentary affliction is preparing for us an eternal weight of glory beyond all comparison, as we look not to the things that are seen but to the things that are unseen. For the things that are seen are transient, but the things that are unseen are eternal. 2 Corinthians 4:16–18, emphasis added

* * * *

What we see in the mirror is transient. Changing. We can remain an aging adult who seems content to rust away in self-focused reflections, complaints, and cynical thoughts or decide *(a choice that results in action)* to join a growing number of people who are active seniors. Embracing a new way of living.

These active seniors are sometimes called "productive seniors" because being productive is what they are. No matter their limitations, they have engaged life and are determined to live life fully within their physical and mental boundaries.

Rarely do we find them at home unless they enjoy gardening, painting, writing, or pursuing other mind-enriching hobbies. Yes, they have their share of scars and bruises of life, physical afflictions, and other annoying problems of aging. However, they are committed not to allow these things prevent their golf games, swimming, working out at the gym, running marathons, leisure travel, or volunteer work. They are committed life-long learners, avid book readers, and expert crossword puzzle solvers. They enjoy stimulating conversations and eating together—the list goes on. *Productive seniors all!*

As we age, isolation becomes increasingly easy and often sought. But *Genesis 2:18* tells us that though God was pleased with what He created—it was very good—there was one thing missing. One thing He said was not good: *"It is not good that the man should be alone; I will make a helper fit for him."* Although this verse speaks specifically of God providing a life partner for Adam, it broadly encompasses relationships. Something God enjoys with infinite pleasure within the trinity of His Person. Something that will be fully realized when His children come home to be with Him.

Accepting others is important and beneficial. Being with others is God's intention from the moment we are born. To be with others is a decision of our will. It takes practice for those who do not find being with people instinctively easy. But it's necessary *(Proverbs 18:1)*.

Engage people around you who share a common interest and desire to be with others. Meet regularly with them in age-appropriate venues. We become productive seniors by moving from the rocking chair and *choosing* to embrace others.

We aren't meant to be alone! Determine to meet new people and develop new relationships. Staying in our comfort zone with familiar friends does not motivate us to meet new people. Immersing ourselves in the lives of people around us can be a pleasurable experience and essential as we grow older.

Activities and interests change with time. That's okay! The objective is to stay involved at some appropriate level of enjoyable activity.

Being productive as we age is not only an encouragement for others but stimulates self-confidence and contributes to personal worth. It may, in fact, free us from those pesky aches and pains. Be prepared to pepper these new relationships with acts of kindness. As God freely gives to us, we can give to others. The important thing is to know we *can* do it. *Yes. We can! "I can do all things through him who strengthens me" (Philippians 4:13).*

Accepting Joyfully Who We Are

Being joyful comes from a peaceful and thankful heart. Such a heart reflects our relationship with God and how well we accept ourselves as someone designed for His purpose. Daily, He gifts us with His love, grace, and kindness. Get moving and start living again in the freshness of His presence in our lives. As His child, we are royalty. Begin to think and behave like those with a special relationship with the King. We are blessed forever by God! *Wow!*

So, take a new grip with your tired hands and strengthen your weak knees. Mark out a straight path for your feet so that those who are weak, and lame will not fall but become strong. Work at living in peace with everyone, and work at living a holy life, for those who are not holy will not see the Lord. Hebrews 12:12–14, NLT

But you are a chosen race, a royal priesthood, a holy nation, a people for his own possession, that you may proclaim the excellencies of him who called you out of darkness into his marvelous light. Once you were not a people, but now you are God's people; once you had not received mercy, but now you have received mercy.
1 Peter 2:9–10

As we age, our relationship with God is easily forgotten. Maybe it was in Sunday School many years ago as a child when we first heard about God's love. Whenever that was, build a memory bridge back to that event. Take a journey across the bridge of past years and rummage through the thoughts of experiences and events. Somewhere, in the land of distant memories, on the other side of the bridge, there was God with His invitation of love in Christ. Recall His voice, "Follow Me!" *What has become of that memory?*

Although we may have forgotten, He hasn't forgotten. God's love for us is intense and hasn't diminished with time. Let's remember what we may have overlooked from earlier years. Accepting ourselves is incomplete without accepting and embracing God. Accepting Him as our loving Father is only through Jesus Christ, God's Son.

God so loved the world that He gave His only Son that whoever believes in Him will not perish but have everlasting life. John 3:16

Many folks, in their old age, refuse to accept the gift God has given them. By rejecting the gift, they reject the Giver. There is no other thing or person that can bring us to the Father except believing in Jesus. Through His gift of forgiveness, He made it possible to enjoy God forever. He is the ultimate gift to accept. But the choice is ours, even in our old age! *It's never too late!*

Fulfillment, joy, and thankfulness result from accepting God's ultimate gift. Each day becomes a new beginning for those who know they are God's loved possession through Christ. *Enjoy the day!*

Since they know their future is secure, they continue to be thankful for everything, no matter what life has in store for them. They have heaven's song in their hearts and upon their lips. Prayer becomes their breath of life and the Bible their daily comfort as they listen to God's voice.

Coming together for Bible study and prayer, their joy and thankfulness fill the room with the presence of Jesus. What a delight they are to be with.

With renewed purpose, they are anxious to promote Christ's coming kingdom. They fill their lives with activities that produce eternal dividends beyond their lifetime. While seeking the welfare of others, heaven is their focus. Be sure to read the story of Myrna at the end of Chapter 3, page 73.

Let's accept life as God has planned it, not as we want it. The gift of aging is beautiful, leading to a fulfilled life with purpose and peace. It's God's gift to us. Let's remember to say, "Thank you," the next time we see ourselves in the mirror! Accept His gift of aging.

I will sing of your strength, in the morning I will sing of your love; for you are my fortress, my refuge in times of trouble. O my Strength, I sing praise to you; you, O God, are my fortress, my loving God. Psalm 59:16–17

Allow Your Servant

Oh my God, my King – Allow your servant

To accept the days appointed to him,

With hands full of purpose

And a heart full of love

For my Master and Friend.

—Don Zoller, 2005

Let's Talk About It

1. *What do you see when looking into your mirror? Is there a difference in how you perceive yourself and the image you see? Describe that difference.*

2. *Do you accept what you see honestly, gracefully, and with thanksgiving? If not, what are the issues?*

3. *Is being old an unwanted burden, or are you generally at peace with your age? Describe how you came to peace with your old age.*

4. *How do you avoid the "Dark Side of The Mirror?"*

5. *What activities keep you curious, flexible, and passionate about life as an older person?*

6. *Are you enjoying the enduring gift of aging with a positive, personal, and growing relationship with Jesus? Describe your experience.*

The LORD your God is in your midst, a mighty one who will save; He will rejoice over you with gladness. He will quiet you by His love; He will exult over you with loud singing. Zephaniah 3:17

Looking Ahead

In our next chapter, we will look at the challenge of *Memories* as we age. We reflect on life's journey by cherishing precious memories. Like pictures in a photo album, memories tell much about who we were, people we knew, and places we remember. However, some memories are blurred and need discarding. Those that only weigh us down. When used correctly, we will learn how memories are a special gift from God to encourage us and others.

2

Memories

Memories are like pictures in a photo album. As with photo albums, memories are a collection of mental images of the past — the people, places, and events we remember. Each memory is a snapshot that captures a moment in time. And each has a story to be told. As with any photo album, we like to preserve the good memories and delete the bad ones that are blurred and distorted. Often, these memories rehearse unwanted pain and grief. Such memories are a challenge as we age.

In this Chapter, we will discuss how memories affect our lives. We will learn how to manage our memories while discovering how God uses them for intended blessings. Come along and find out what to remember and what to forget.

A Precious Treasure

M ost memories are precious treasures. As we grow older, these unique treasures become more valuable. Priceless. Such memories become the stories frequently told and retold on the stage of our mind. And, perhaps, rehearsed (more than once) for others. *"Ah, yes! I remember when . . . "*

Memories of family—children, pets, vacations, places, and special events are woven into the intricate tapestry of a satisfied life. The smell of ocean mist, the scent of pine trees on a gentle mountain slope, or the enchanting fragrance of flowers in bloom—all captured in the photo album of our memories. The summer breeze on its journey across an open field, birds in flight as they sing to one another, the warmth of a campfire freely sending its embers upward—these create the stage for a delightful collection of memories. Beautifully composed photos of the mind.

There can also be memories of a deceased husband or wife. Reflections of happy moments spent as a loving couple venturing through life together. Times of intimacy, beauty, and joy. But there were also tough, difficult, and challenging times. However, with each, we remember how we managed to work through them together. Cherished memories held in the recesses of our hearts as precious treasures secured within the hallowed sanctuaries of the past.

In solitude, perhaps at the close of day, thoughts of our past come alive as the sun casts its long shadows upon life around us. Our mind's artistic skill paints the panorama of bygone years in glorious color. From somewhere in the distant past, faces and words of our loved ones are invited into the present and given life in the photo album of our memory. Some may call this daydreaming. For others, it is simply a pleasant stroll down memory lane. *Memories—they are who God made us to be. What a wonderful treasure they are!*

Other Kinds of Memories

Some memories protect us from present dangers, unwanted words, actions from our past, and foolish behaviors. Our memories don't easily forget the pain of a sharp edge, an electrical shock, or possibly a deep hurt inflicted by careless words. A healthy memory will use unpleasant moments to remind us not to repeat what previously caused pain and harm.

Falling is always a possibility, particularly as we age. Once we have had a couple of falls, maybe serious ones, our memory recalls the dangers that abound each time we start to walk. Memory is our safeguard against accidental falls and other misadventures. Given the opportunity, memories from the past keep us safe in the present. *Don't do that anymore.*

Memories help us remember names we have forgotten. Forgetting people's names is awkward and embarrassing at any age. But forgetting becomes more common as we age. If we forget, just ask! People are happy to help. *Remember, most have the same problem!*

Memories are challenged. Whether forgetting people's names, items we forgot at the grocery store, or remembering where we are going, memory blackouts happen. We can't remember. It's a missing photo in our photo album. Like a computer that loses memory, our memory goes blank. Information gone! This situation becomes an embarrassing challenge.

We live in an information-saturated society with visual and audio overloads on every hand. We try to remember numbers, birthdates, names, PINs, passwords, and passcodes in one form or another. Add to this complex world TVs, phones, and computers that require so much more of our memory capacity. A severe challenge to overworked and tired memories. One elderly woman said, "I forget half of what I am supposed to remember, and the other half, I've forgotten what I already remembered."

Moments of forgetfulness are a shared experience among older adults. If we sense our memory becoming fuzzy, we are not alone. This forgetfulness is probably not cognitive impairment, such as dementia, but rather a tired brain, worn out and overloaded from working overtime most of its life. The memory now challenged to do more with less ability to remember the overwhelming demands of today's world.

Don't depend on instant recall. Attempting on-the-spot recall is a sure way to encounter memory failure. Many memory tools on the Internet or phone apps help us remember things that need to be remembered.

However, a great way to begin our day and help our memory is in quietness with the Lord. Think calmly and prayerfully about the day, where we will go, what we will say, and the people, places, and events we will encounter. Use a scratch pad or iPhone Notes app to map and shape the day. Then, use these notes throughout the day as needed. They will help our challenged memory recall the important things. Your memory will thank you. Oh, yes. One more thing: hold your plans lightly. Remember, God is sovereign. *We can make our plans, but the LORD determines our steps (Proverbs 16:9, NLT).*

Abusing Your Memory

Like a photo album filled with images of people, places, and events from the past, some memories fade, become blurred, and distorted. Some memories rekindle the pain and grief we want to forget. As with anything of value, memories can be abused.

At times, distorted memories become the measure of what life *should be* today and isn't. Those who immerse themselves in the past may complain that things today are not how they were. They become cynical and distrustful of the present. *"Well, in my day, we did not . . ."*

Being preoccupied with a distorted view of the past is not a healthy use of a God-given memory. The past can become a self-created fantasy that never existed. It is possible to become so rooted in the past that we no longer want to live in the present emotionally. Living excessively in the past is memory abuse. *"After all, life was so much better then."*

We remember the fish we ate in Egypt that cost nothing, the cucumbers, the melons, the leeks, the onions, and the garlic. But now our strength is dried up, and there is nothing at all but this manna to look at. Numbers 11:5–6

Another form of memory abuse is to focus on photos of past tragedies, violence, emotional pain, severe trauma, and broken relationships. When we eliminate God from these stories, when they are not seen from His perspective, and when the healing ointment of His love is not applied, scars and a disfigured memory remain. Yes. These memories still hurt. And some hurt a whole lot. But God is ever present to wipe away the tears and comfort the aching heart if we surrender these negative memories to Him.

Spending time in guilt for past sinful behavior can be another form of memory abuse. We may become enslaved to these discolored memories, carrying the weight of past guilt into the present. In lonely moments, such memories haunt older people. Often, they cry, *"Oh, how I wish it could have been different."*

In the following section, we will see how God has dealt with the guilt of the past. *It's amazing!*

Remember and Remember Not

Finally, brothers, whatever is true, whatever is honorable, whatever is just, whatever is pure, whatever is lovely, whatever is commendable, if there is any excellence, if there is anything worthy of praise, think about these things.
Philippians 4:8

Some memories are worth remembering, and some are not. Memories that give peace and comfort to the soul, calm a stressful mind, and quiet an agitated spirit are to be remembered. Learn to use them in difficult moments. These memories give us strength and encouragement. *"Wait a minute! This problem isn't that bad. I remember how God . . . "*

Glory in his holy name; let the hearts of those who seek the LORD rejoice! Seek the LORD and his strength; seek his presence continually! **<u>Remember</u> (put into your memory for instant recall)** *the wondrous works that he has done, his miracles, and the judgments he uttered.*

1 Chronicles 16:10–12, emphasis added

But there are harmful, abusive memories we may want to forget. These are easy to detect. They tear us down. They produce stress, inner turmoil, and despair, resurrecting the pain of the past. Most importantly, they harm our relationship with God. We become self-focused rather than Christ-focused. They have no redemptive value. With negative memories, we separate ourselves from God, who constantly seeks our welfare, peace, and blessing.

Remember not the former things, nor consider the things of old. Behold, I am doing a new thing; now it springs forth, do you not perceive it? I will make a way in the wilderness and rivers in the desert.   *Isaiah 43:18–19*

Only God knows how to sort through our photo album. He alone can determine what is of value to keep. He will use both good and bad memories for His purpose. But some memories have no divine purpose and must be discarded. Only the Holy Spirit, through the Word of God and prayer, is wise enough to do the editing.

But God may not remove all unpleasant memories. Some He will preserve for His purposes. As we surrender these negative memories, He transforms them for our good. Overwhelming us with His love. Such memories draw us more passionately to Christ.

You will keep in perfect peace all who trust in you, all whose thoughts are fixed on you! Trust in the LORD always, for the LORD GOD is the eternal Rock.
Isaiah 26:3-4 (NLT

Create in me a clean heart, O God, and renew a steadfast spirit within me. Psalm 51:10

A God-Blessed Memory

Before meeting Jesus on the Damascus Road, the Apostle Paul persecuted the church—those who followed Jesus. He threw many into prison, assigning them to pain, suffering, and death. Paul had blood on his hands. But all that changed when he met Jesus.

No, dear brothers and sisters . . . I focus on this one thing: Forgetting the past and looking forward to what lies ahead, I press on to reach the end of the race and receive the heavenly prize for which God, through Christ Jesus, is calling us. Philippians 3:13–14, NLT

Paul did not rethink his past. He looked forward to what lay ahead. *And so must we!* Paul had neither time nor desire to look back at what he used to be. Paul's new life began when he encountered Jesus on the Damascus Road. He did not hesitate when he said,

> *Therefore, if anyone is in Christ, he is a new creation. The old has passed away; behold, the new has come. All this is from God. 2 Corinthians 5:17–18, emphasis added*

When Jesus gathered with His disciples in the Upper Room at the Last Supper, He spoke of His sacrificial death on a cross. He told them, "Remember Me." *Don't forget Me.* Without question, these two words are foundational to our lives as His followers. these two simple words define a reference point for all we think, say, or do: "Remember Me." These words are to be etched deeply into our memories. God's Word requires that we remember the things He has revealed.

Yet, His Word also compels us to remember what God has forgotten!

> *I am He who blots out your transgressions for my own sake, and I will not remember your sins. Isaiah 43:25, emphasis added*

> *For I will forgive their iniquity, and I will remember their sin no more." Jeremiah 31:34 emphasis added*

Jesus' sacrifice on the cross was complete, never to be repeated. Dear older brother or sister in Christ, remember that God has *forgotten* your past sin, draining dry the pool of guilt as His Word affirms. Since God had forgotten them, *so must you!*

Sins that trouble our memory are removed from God's memory. They no longer exist. They are gone as far as the east is from the west *(Psalm103:11-14)*. Our sins are *forgiven, forgotten, forever, Amen.*

Therefore, lift your drooping hands and strengthen your weak knees, and make straight paths for your feet, so that what is lame may not be put out of joint but rather be healed.
Hebrews 12:12–13

Let us daily thank the Lord for our minds and the precious memories it contains. A God-blessed memory can also encourage others who struggle with their photo album of unwanted memories. *Memories imprinted with God's love are a true treasure from Him! It is His gift to you.*

Psalm 103:14

For he knows how weak we are;
he remembers we are only dust. (NLT)

Let's Talk About It

1. *What do your memories mean to you? Are they cherished landscapes of beauty, giving tranquility to the soul, or do they bring pain and grief? Explain.*

2. *How have your memories protected you from present dangers and harm?*

3. *How do you deal with unwanted memories?*

4. *How do your memories help or limit you in your older years?*

5. *How do you discipline your mind to remember the good memories and discard those that should be forgotten?*

6. *Do you rest comfortably with the words "Forgiven, forgotten, forever, Amen" when they refer to your past sins? If not, explain.*

For behold, I create new heavens and a new earth, and the former things shall not be remembered or come into mind. But be glad and rejoice forever in that which I create; for behold, I create Jerusalem to be a joy, and her people to be a gladness. Isaiah 65:17–18

Looking Ahead

In our next Chapter, we will consider the challenge of *Suffering*. We will discover God's purpose for our suffering while acknowledging the pain, grief, and misery that our suffering often brings. We will see how it is possible to glorify Him while suffering. We will also discover God's secret to suffering. *Joy!*

A Deeper Sound

Oh, a deeper sound the note must make,
Of love's sweet song for God alone.
No surface noise can replicate
The Healing Hand upon the soul.

Carefully, Lord, You have wounded me,
That the fragrance of the broken
Be to You an offering — a pleasant thing,
Of love's deeper sound for You alone.

Healing ointment my Great Physician brings,
To correct, instruct, and bless;
To tune the note for the deeper sound,
Of love's sweet song for God alone.

—Don Zoller, 1986

Suffering

Suffering is a significant part of living, particularly in our journey of aging. For many, it is overwhelming. Often, we experience suffering as an interruption or an intrusion. Painful and unwanted. But God, in His providence, divinely crafts our suffering to wean us from the world's attractions to woo us to the presence of Christ. Let's find out how the challenge of suffering can be God's special gift to us. A gift of joy!

A healthy person has a thousand wishes.
A sick person has only one. A Proverb

When suffering shatters the carefully kept vase
that is our lives, God stoops down to pick up the pieces.
But He doesn't put them back together as a restoration
project patterned after our former selves.
Instead, He sifts through the rubble and selects
some of the shards as new material for another
project—a mosaic that tells the story of redemption.
—Ken Gire, The North Face of God

S uffering is universal. Everyone has experienced it. No one wants it! Each can describe this unwanted experience in their own terms. Beyond discomfort caused by pain, grief, and misery are the inner struggles of mind and spirit. Suffering consumes who we are and distorts what we need to be.

Suffering is not generally a popular topic for casual conversation. It is politely avoided. When we ask, "How are you?" a common reply is, "I'm okay" or "Just fine, thanks." Inquiry to delve deeper beyond this response is usually considered inappropriate.

Thus, we may never hear what lies below the waterline of hurt and pain. Where the real battle with suffering rages. Reluctant to share with others, only their doctor, pastor, or counselor may know the extent of their pain and grief.

The news media presents a world that is overwhelmed by suffering. But suffering is not an abstract idea but a personal experience. It is about people. And it infuses all of creation.

For we know that the whole creation has been groaning together in the pains of childbirth until now. Romans 8:22

The ravages of war, violence, natural disasters, social injustices, broken relationships, loss of loved ones, accidents, illnesses, and more all scream of hurting people. People suffering. Eight billion people who occupy today's world know, in some measure, the pain of suffering.

Suffering began with our first parents in the Garden of Eden *(Genesis 3:16–19)*. It is a common theme throughout Scripture and occupies much of secular drama, literature, and the daily media. Unavoidable suffering defines the pain and grief that permeates our human experience.

Suffering is particularly acute for older people as strength in their bodies diminishes and their minds weaken. Chronic weakness, fatigue, and illness often overwhelm them. *They're wearing out.*

As one who experiences these undeniable features of growing old, I found a book encouraging me to care for an aging body and mind. *Living Younger Longer* by

Stephen Kopecky, M.D., is an excellent book written in layman's language. A Mayo Clinic cardiologist and two-time cancer survivor, the book is highly recommended by healthcare professionals and available at Mayo Clinic Press or online.[5]

The Box on Our Doorstep

A box arrives on our doorstep. It's addressed to us with a label, "Suffering Just for You!" At some point in our lives, we all receive this box, probably more than once. No one is exempt from suffering. No one can escape it. It reaches out to all of us. In small ways or in ways that can be devastating. At times, life-threatening.

Here it is, on our doorstep. Unwanted. Something we never ordered or expected. Its arrival may even surprise us. It soon becomes apparent we cannot "return to sender." We have no choice but to open it. There it is! All the suffering we *never* wanted.

Yet physical pain, emotional stress, and grief are to be expected in our fallen world. Living a life free of suffering, at least for very long, is unrealistic. We're going to hurt. And sometimes, a whole lot!

For affliction does not come from the dust, nor does trouble sprout from the ground, but man is born to trouble as the sparks fly upward. Job 5:6–7

What has a man from all the toil and striving of heart with which he toils beneath the sun? For all his days are full of sorrow, and his work is a vexation. Even in the night his heart does not rest. This also is vanity. Ecclesiastes 2:22

For some, suffering is occasional. For others, chronic, with only rare moments when it doesn't hurt. Remember, we are not alone when the box of unwanted suffering lands on our doorstep. *We all suffer.*

Man, who is born of a woman is few of days and full of trouble. Job 14:1b

However, we may fail to see that our box of suffering is what God will use to bless us and glorify Himself as He transforms it into *a gift*. It's how we receive our box that makes the difference.

Instinctively, we gravitate toward an inward-looking, self-absorbed posture. "Why me?" Someone else or thing is to blame. It hurts, and we don't like it. But here is the challenge: the Bible says we are to receive suffering with *joy!*

Count it all joy, my brothers, when you meet trials of various kinds for you know that the testing of your faith produces steadfastness. And let steadfastness have its full effect, that you may be perfect and complete, lacking in nothing. James 1:2-4

"Counting it all joy" may taunt us when overwhelmed by suffering. A big leap from suffering to joy. But read on to discover how God helps us do just that.

Suffering is About Loss

Suffering can mean the loss of health, wealth, and relationships. Sometimes all three. It's about the pain, trauma, anxiety, and depression that loss ushers into our lives. Suffering is also about the loss we experience through rejection and persecution as followers of Jesus *(Philippians 1:29)*. It's all there, in the box on our doorstep.

In the opening chapters of the Book of Job, we read about a morally upright and devoted man of God. Job worshipped God and prayed for his family. God was pleased with Job and blessed him with wealth and notoriety *(Job 1:1–5)*.

His favored life, however, did not protect him from overwhelming suffering. Job lost everything: his health, wealth, and family. And he experienced rejection—verbal hostility from his wife and friends *(Job 1:13–19, 2:7-10)*. Job is the classic example of why good people suffer.

Understanding how Job handled suffering when it arrived on his doorstep will help us deal with it when it touches our lives. He did three things.

First, he humbled himself. He neither resisted the heavy hand of God nor accused God of wrongdoing. Second, he worshipped God. And third, he allowed God's sovereignty to embrace him and acknowledged God was in control and sole owner of everything in creation. He could rightfully do whatever He wanted (Job 1:21–22; 2:10).

Applying Job's three-fold response to our experience is a significant step toward learning to suffer God's way—a way that recognizes suffering as a gift.

Jesus, in the Garden of Gethsemane, gives us further insight into suffering. There in the Garden—the Garden of Surrender—He faced the reality of crucifixion: public humiliation, torture, unimaginable suffering, and death. Jesus fell to the ground and humbly surrendered Himself to the Father's will. "Not my will, but yours be done." In great agony of spirit, he poured out His soul before His Father, sweating drops of blood. Why did Jesus suffer so greatly?

The Bible teaches that Jesus, although fully God, was also fully man. As man, He willingly took our grief and suffering upon Himself to accomplish His Father's will. He would become God's sacrificial lamb for us (Hebrews 2:10, Isaiah 53:3–5).

When we struggle with suffering and loss, it's easy to accuse God for our pain. Releasing our will to the

Father, as Jesus did, is a further step in our journey toward counting it all joy. But surrendering our will to God's purpose is not easy.

We may need to surrender our will more than once during our suffering. Yes, it's who we are. But it's also how we grow in our journey of *counting it all joy*. A journey that begins and ends with faith. Trusting God, who promises to be with us in our season of suffering.

"The will of God is never exactly what you expect it to be. It may be much worse, but in the end, it's going to be a lot better and a lot bigger." —Elisabeth Elliot,[6] *(whose husband was killed while serving as a missionary in Ecuador)*

In faith, enter the garden of surrender where Jesus suffered. There, experience His presence in your suffering and loss. And receive His comfort, peace, and strength to endure. Kneel with Him as He invites you to humbly submit to His Father and say, *"Not my will, but yours be done."*

Remember, He knows us intimately and loves us intensely. Jesus said that no one (nothing) can remove us from the Father's protective hand of love *(John 10:28–29)*. No matter how long or severe our suffering or how vocal our pain, God's love toward us is never diminished. Nothing, not even the agony of our pain, can separate us from His love

For I am sure that neither death nor life, nor angels nor rulers, nor things present nor things to come, nor powers, nor height nor depth, nor anything else in all creation, will be able to separate us from the love of God in Christ Jesus our Lord. Romans 8:38–39

Yes, suffering is a time of great loss, but it can also be a time of great gain if we submit to the One who knows and controls what is in our box.

Indeed, I count everything as loss because of the surpassing worth of knowing Christ Jesus my Lord. For his sake I have suffered the loss of all things and count them as rubbish, in order that I may gain Christ. Philippians 3:8

Appendix 1, page 183, is a short story about Aggie Hurst. It beautifully illustrates how God takes our great loss, despair, and suffering and transforms it into great gain and blessing for His glory.

Appendix 2, page 191, follows with a poem that reaches out to those who suffer—the Wounded, Forsaken, Broken—along their journey on *The Longest Road.*

* * * *

But Why Me?

Have we ever asked, "Why me?" These may be the first words out of our mouth when suffering suddenly devours our lives. Taking a quick inventory of our lives, we may conclude with Job, "I've done nothing wrong." "My relationship with God appears to be okay." "What have I done to deserve this?" "Where is God in all of this, especially when I need Him most?" "Why me?"

Although a frequent reaction to suffering, a "Why me?" question points us in the wrong direction. "Why me?" points to *me*. It makes me of primary importance. Our suffering becomes self-absorbing, erasing a proper understanding of God's way.

"Why me?" distorts our perspective of God. We may decide God doesn't know what He is doing or isn't in control of our situation. Perhaps He doesn't care that we are suffering. It becomes easy to find fault with God. We may reason that if God is truly the One who loves me, why am I suffering?

A Bible story provides insight into the dilemma of "Why me? *John 11:1–44* records the death of Lazarus, a good friend of Jesus. We learn that Jesus loved Lazarus and his two sisters, Mary and Martha. They were intimate friends. Lazarus became seriously sick and died within a few days. But after hearing of the illness of Lazarus, Jesus remained where He was two days longer, seemingly unconcerned about His friend. Only when He knew that Lazarus was dead did He and His disciples journey to Bethany, the home of Mary and Martha.

Their brother's death was devastating to Mary and Martha. They not only lost their brother, whom they loved, but they were now destitute and faced inevitable poverty. And, from their perspective, Jesus didn't seem to care. He was *four days* late.

In their sorrow, the sisters could only express the anguish of their disappointment with Jesus. "Where were you, Jesus, when we needed you—while our brother was still alive? He would still be with us if you had been here." "Why are you putting us through all this pain and suffering?" *"Why us, the ones you said you loved?"*

How could Jesus possibly be so unloving and insensitive in a time of such dire suffering? Didn't He care? Yes, Jesus was *four days* late, but not according to God's clock; He was right on time. *"It is for the glory of God, so that the Son of God may be glorified through it."* (*John 11:4*).

God used the death of Lazarus to reveal His glory not just to Mary and Martha but to untold millions who, to this day, desperately need the same words of hope Jesus gave them, *"I am the resurrection and life"* (*John 11:25–26*). This hope comes from a merciful God to all who suffer, who are willing to leave behind the question, "Why me?" God is never late or unconcerned in revealing Himself in your suffering. His plan is always bigger than our "Why me?"

In our suffering, God provides Himself as the strength we need to endure. As our loving comforter and counselor, He reveals His glory. When adversity strikes, God seeks us more than we seek Him.

God is always excited about His glory and wants His children to experience it. Admittedly, we have little idea what sharing in God's glory means. Still, it was one of the last things Jesus wished for us before His death on the cross *(John 17:24)*. Our ability to enjoy Christ's glory is inseparably connected to our present suffering *(Romans 8:16-17; 2 Corinthians 4:16–18)*. With this in view, we are getting closer to *"counting it all joy"* and seeing what is in our box of suffering can become a gift.

God's desire to show us His glory may be hard to appreciate, especially when suffering causes pain, grief, and loss. But "Why me?" becomes a distant whisper of insignificance as He infuses His glory into our suffering. A more appropriate question emerges: "How can my suffering honor and glorify God, who, out of His love for me, has allowed this suffering, that His will on earth be done as it is in heaven?"

The story of Lazarus helps us understand another important thing about our suffering. It's possible that our suffering may have little or nothing to do with us.

Our suffering may be the occasion God chooses to accomplish through us something far greater, more far-reaching than our immediate situation. God's ways are beyond our limited understanding. His plan is always bigger than ours. When we fold this thought into our hearts, we move closer to *"counting it all joy."*

Seeking the Father's will and His glory in our suffering—*why would we want anything less?*

And though the Lord give you the bread of adversity and the water of affliction, yet your Teacher will not hide himself anymore, but your eyes shall see your Teacher. And your ears shall hear a word behind you, saying, "This is the way, walk in it," when you turn to the right or when you turn to the left. Isaiah 30:20–21

Why Now?

We dislike interruptions—unplanned intrusions into our neatly arranged lives. Somehow, we make room for them, hoping they will soon disappear. Some interruptions, however, linger.

Suffering is such an interruption. It never consults our schedule. As an inconvenient and untimely "guest," suffering arrives unannounced and intends to stay, disrupting our plans, meetings, and commitments.

Suffering upsets everything it touches, oblivious to our projects, planned gatherings with family and friends, travel, business, or church-related activities. It doesn't care that people are depending on us. Suffering destroys our well-ordered lives.

"Why now?" "I am too busy to deal with this kind of interruption." But listen to the words of Scripture, *"For everything there is a season, and a time for every matter under the sun" (Ecclesiastes 3:1).*

The writer of Ecclesiastes sees life differently than we often do. *Ecclesiastes 3:2–8* captures the changing seasons of human experiences—a time for everything, including suffering. The rhythm and order of life's seasons do not anticipate the question, "Why now?" Although we may react to suffering as an interruption, suffering is understood by the writer of Ecclesiastes as a necessary part of our faith-walk with Christ *(I Peter 1:6–7).*

God sees the sum of our lives comprised of various events under His control, including our seasons of suffering. Our suffering is not an interruption but essential to His purpose for our ultimate blessing and His glory.

As the Apostle Paul, a man of great zeal and energy, traveled to Damascus, Jesus struck him blind. Now transformed and a chosen instrument, Jesus charged him to make known His name before the Gentiles, kings, and the children of Israel *(Acts 9:15).*

What a calling! What an opportunity! But Jesus added something more: *"I will show him how much he must suffer for my name's sake" (Acts 9:16).*

What's this all about? Time was short. Paul had a vast territory to cover and much work to do, planting and caring for churches in Asia and Europe. And yet, amid such profound work, with so many people depending on him, Paul had to suffer. Paul was far too busy to be interrupted by suffering. But God saw his life differently.

Like Paul, suffering slows us down. It may in fact stop us. Often, suffering removes us from the race and keeps us from doing the "important stuff" of life —even things God may have put in our hands to do for Him. At least, this is how we see it.

But God quietly reminds us, *"Your life, including your service for Me, is not really about you. It's about Me and My glory."* The simple truth is that God's ways are not our ways, and neither are our thoughts His thoughts. It seems He has a different way of doing things.

For Paul, this meant imprisonments and beatings. Near-death experiences, lashes, rods, and stoning, He was shipwrecked three times, suffered hunger, sleepless nights, and much more *(2 Corinthians 11:23–29).*

But that was not enough. God added another layer of suffering to Paul's life—*a thorn* (Gk: *skolopsa* a stake, i.e., tent peg) in the flesh. It hurt so much that he asked the Lord *three times* (Heb fig: ceaselessly, many) to remove it. Yet God denied his persistent requests. God's reply gave Paul the answer for his pain and suffering: *"My grace is sufficient for you, for my power is made perfect in weakness" (2 Corinthians 12:7–10).* God's answer to Paul helps to clarify our questions when we suffer as He intervenes to reveal His power and grace.

Paul learned an important lesson that applies to us. Our life doesn't depend on us for its success, significance, or timely outcomes. Our life is God's work, executed and empowered by His Spirit *(Zechariah 4:6). His work is always much, much bigger than you or I can ever imagine.* He sees not only the stage upon which we stand, but He knows the entire performance—how it begins and how it ends. He sees what we cannot see. He knows what is impossible for us to know.

Learning to suffer God's way means we must leave behind our "Why now?" as we pursue our journey toward *"counting it all joy."*

"Why me?" and "Why now?" are self-absorbing questions that get in the way of what God wants to accomplish through our suffering. He seeks to show His love for us in unique and special ways. He wants to make His presence a faith reality during our pain. He wants us to grow in our relationship with Him and make room for Him in our suffering!

But Why Not?

God likes to ask questions, too. Being prone to ask, "Why me?" and "Why now?" when suffering arrives on our doorstep, He is ready with His question, *"Why not?"* After all, He is in charge of His creation from the farthest star to the smallest element in the atom within our body. He orchestrates every detail of life, every breath we breathe, and every step we take. His creation, including you and me, is subject to His direction as He moves everything from time toward eternity. If He determines that a season of suffering will further His glory and bring to us His blessing, and perhaps to others, then "Why not?"

Job and others in the Bible understood that God is sovereign, meaning everything and everyone is subject to Him. *"Shall we receive good from God, and shall we not receive evil?"* (Job 2:10)

Nebuchadnezzar, king of Babylon, restored by God to a sound mind, clearly saw God for who He is. One who does what He wants, when He wants, and how He wants—without question *(Daniel 4:34–35)*. The Psalmist declared, *"Our God is in the heavens; He does all that He pleases" (Psalm 115:3).* And, whatever God pleases, He does for His glory.

While we suffer, we may disagree with God about His sovereignty. However, agreeing with God about what pleases Him, even in our season of suffering, brings us closer to counting it all joy. When we suffer God's way, His love and grace become interwoven into our experience.

In response, such love and grace bubble over into our worship, thanksgiving, and praise to God. This experience is what brings glory to Him and joy to us. If bringing glory to Him is our greatest desire, why would we not want to agree with God when He asks, "Why not?"

So we do not lose heart. Though our outer self is wasting away, our inner self is being renewed day by day. For this light momentary affliction is preparing for us an eternal weight of glory beyond all comparison, as we look not to the things that are seen but to the things that are unseen. For the things that are seen are transient, but the things that are unseen are eternal. 2 Corinthians 4:16–18

Why Am I Suffering

When life hits us hard, we try to make sense of it, particularly when it affects our health, wealth, or relationships. Having put aside the questions of "Why me?" and "Why now?" there remains yet another question in keeping with God's purposes. "Why am I suffering?"

This question is not another way of asking, "Why me?" but a time to engage God to show us the purpose for our suffering. To take a deeper look at our suffering. Is God grabbing our attention to follow Christ more closely? To nurture our relationships with others differently? To seek a new direction for our lives?

These and other questions are appropriate during or after our season of suffering. God may show us His purpose. However, He is not obligated to give us a reason. Why we suffer may remain unknown and unseen. The unknown and unseen is where trust in His goodness comes in. He knows what He is doing in ways that may give us no answers. That's okay. Be at peace and allow faith to rest in His silence.

Suffering became part of the human experience at the beginning—*Genesis 3:16–19*. As a product of the curse, we experience disease, accidents, brokenness, grief and deterioration of an aging body or mind. Adverse events beyond our control. It was not met to be that way.

Suffering may be corrective, punitive, or a means to strengthen our faith. Suffering may be collective such as famines, plagues, wars, or natural disasters in which entire communities suffer. Or none of the above.

Regardless of the reason for suffering, it can only come to us as God allows it to happen *(Deuteronomy 32:39; Lamentations 3:31–33)*. The answer to our "Why am I suffering?" may not be immediate. It may not come at all. God never told Job why he was suffering. Sometimes, God's answer to this question remains with Him. Trust in God, not the answer.

However, there is one reason the Bible explicitly gives for our suffering:

> *Blessed be the God and Father of our Lord Jesus Christ, the Father of mercies and God of all comfort, who comforts us in all our affliction, so that we may be able to comfort those who are in any affliction, with the comfort with which we ourselves are comforted by God. For as we share abundantly in Christ's sufferings, so through Christ we share abundantly in comfort too. 2 Corinthians 1:3–5*

Based on this verse, there is at least one reason for our suffering. While we are suffering, we can comfort others as they suffer. In our suffering, we may be the one God calls to encourage and give hope to another who is suffering. Amid our grief, we can reflect God's love and peace to the one in need, thus counting it all joy. It's another way to see the glory of God.

Our suffering may allow others to experience God. We may not want to pray or read our Bible when suffering. However, others who love and care for us are encouraged to pray and read from the Scriptures on our behalf. They can also meet our physical needs—prepare food, do the laundry, run errands, or make phone calls.

As they serve us, God blesses them. Don't discourage their acts of giving. It's important for them, it's important to us, and it's important to God as we allow them to serve us. It can be a time of healing for all of us. This is how the body of Christ is supposed to work.

Counting it all joy is rooted in our relationship with God. Without this relationship, anchored by our faith in Jesus Christ, there can be no joy, peace, or hope in suffering. Sin is the disabling factor that prevents us from experiencing the fullness of joy in our suffering. But Jesus has removed our sin forever so that we may enjoy His presence and joy *(John 15:11; 17:24)*.

Although we may not know why we suffer, we have the eternal assurance of God's Word that He is faithful. His love for us will not allow our weakness to be tested beyond His power to keep us. He will never forsake us!

"Why am I suffering?" may have several, few, or no answers. Answers may be immediate, delayed, or never. It's all about trust. Learning to suffer God's way is a journey of personal faith and trust in what we cannot touch, see, or measure.

When you pass through the waters, I will be with you; and through the rivers, they shall not overwhelm you; when you walk through fire you shall not be burned, and the flame shall not consume you. Isaiah 43:2

* * * *

A Second Look

Our journey began when a box arrived on our doorstep—a box we didn't want. A box filled with suffering. But, as we have seen, it is a box delivered by a Friend who loves us with an everlasting love that never forsakes us.

We looked inside our box and experienced the discomfort of its contents. We wrestled and struggled with its pain. We tried to make sense of it. Although we are on a journey to learn how to suffer God's way, it's still hard and perhaps hurts a lot. When we approach suffering like Job, Paul, and Jesus, it's still as painful for us as it was for them. *It isn't easy.*

Although God allows grief, pain, and suffering for His purpose, bathed in His intense love for us, He is forever the God of abundant compassion and mercy.

For the Lord will not cast off forever, but, though he causes grief, he will have compassion according to the abundance of his steadfast love; for he does not willingly (Heb: arbitrarily) afflict or grieve the children of men." Lamentations 3:31–33, emphasis added

God remembers who we are *(Psalm 139:13–16)*. We are not super-people with great endurance, strength, or fortitude. When illness strikes, we become instantly aware of how fragile and brittle we are. Just clay pots. We break easily! Therefore,

As a father shows compassion to his children, so the Lord shows compassion to those who fear him. For he knows our frame; he remembers that we are dust. Psalm 103:13–14

At the graveside of His friend, Jesus wept. And so do we when the life of our loved one ends in death. When there is no one to intervene or provide understanding. No one, except Jesus! Death is the great enemy He defeated at the cross for us. With the death of Lazarus, He saw beyond the immediate to His victory over sin and death as the Resurrection and the Life. Amid our tears, count it all joy! *(1 Thessalonians 4:13)*

We may not have noticed, but something else in the box has been there all along. It's included in every box. Hidden and buried when suffering first arrives. It is something God provides for us when we need it most. His personal handkerchief—monogrammed with His name. *It's for you! In love, He sends His Spirit to comfort you.*

Be sure to look deeply into the box when suffering arrives. God has not forgotten about you.

And I heard a loud voice from the throne saying, Behold, the dwelling place of God is with man. He will dwell with them, and they will be his people, and God himself will be with them as their God. <u>He will wipe away every tear from their eyes</u>, and death shall be no more, neither shall there be mourning, nor crying, <u>nor pain anymore</u>, for the former things have passed away. Revelation 21:3–4, emphasis added

The End of Our Journey—Almost!

Challenged by suffering—lingering pain, grief, despair, and unanswered questions—be assured that God is at work in our lives to show us His unfailing love. In our suffering, He graciously seeks us to surrender our wills and reach out by faith to count it all joy. Such an act of faith doesn't deny the pain of our suffering. Instead, it gives suffering a purpose to infuse a mature and steadfast faith in our lives. A faith to walk close to Christ. Knowing this, we count it all joy. By this, we grow to be more like Him.

Now, we come to the end of our journey—almost. "Almost!" because we still have much to learn and *relearn*. Faith and unwavering trust in God's love and eternal purpose must be revisited throughout our lives—relearned once again. But for now, we know how it's done! *Counting it all joy is God's gift of aging.*

Count it all joy, my brothers, when you meet trials of various kinds for you know that the testing of your faith produces steadfastness. And let steadfastness have its full effect, that you may be perfect and complete, lacking in nothing. James 1:2–4

. . . let us run with endurance the race that is set before us, <u>looking to Jesus</u>, the founder and perfecter of our faith, <u>who for the joy that was set before him endured the cross</u>, despising the shame, and is seated at the right hand of the throne of God. Hebrew 12:1-2, emphasis added

The Story of Madame Guyon

Imprisoned for her faith in Jesus, Madame Guyon (1648–1717) was confined for almost a year to a cell in a dungeon below ground with no windows. Her dark, damp, rat-infested cell reeked with an intolerable stench. Her only light, a candle at mealtimes twice a day. During these brief moments of light, she composed poems and hymns to her Lord. She understood not only why she was suffering, but she adored the One who allowed it. She had learned to suffer God's way by *"counting it all joy."*

A little bird I am,
Shut from the fields of air,
And in my cage, I sit and sing
To Him who placed me there;
Well pleased a prisoner to be,
Because, my God, it pleaseth Thee
Naught have I else to do,
I sing the whole day long;
And He whom most I love to please
Doth listen to my song;
He caught and bound my wandering wing;
But still, He bends to hear me sing.
My cage confines me round;
Abroad, I cannot fly;
But though my wing is closely bound,
My heart's at liberty;
For prison walls cannot control
The flight, the freedom of the soul.

O it is good to soar
These bolts and bars above
To Him whose purpose I adore,
Whose providence I love;
And in Thy mighty will to find
The joy, the freedom of the mine.
Madame Guyon, 1717
Public Domain

Before I was afflicted, I went astray, but now I keep your word . . . It is good for me that I was afflicted. that I might learn your statutes . . . I know, O Lord, that your rules are righteous, and that in faithfulness you have afflicted me. Let your steadfast love comfort me according to your promise to your servant. Let your mercy come to me, that I may live; for your law is my delight. Psalm 119: 67, 71, 75–77

Myrna

Before ending this Chapter, I want to share a personal story about Myrna, an 80+-year-old lady from my church. While I recovered at home from an extended illness, Myrna called promptly at 10:30 every Thursday morning for about three months. With infectious joy, she would blurt, "Well, Don, how are you doing? I hope you are feeling better. How's your strength?" With my health assessment out of the way and a voice filled with laughter, Myrna chatted then shared a verse from Scripture before she prayed. She concluded her phone call by saying, "Thank you. Thank you. Thank you, Jesus."

One day, she missed calling. I called her. Myrna's husband answered. With sadness, he told me Myrna passed away two days earlier from stage four cancer. Myrna suffered severe pain for several months before her death. But now, she was at home with Jesus. Myrna faced her suffering like Job, Paul, and Jesus. She had learned to "count it all joy," and God blessed her while she blessed others, including me. That convinced me that it is possible to suffer God's way and discover purpose in suffering with joy! Join me as we, too, make that discovery.

For I consider that the sufferings of this present time are not worth comparing with the glory that is to be revealed to us. Romans 8:18

Let's Talk About It

1. *How well do you suffer? What things have you learned from your suffering?*

2. *How often do you relate your suffering to God's purposes when afflicted in your body, mind, or spirit?*

3. *Have you ever said, "Thank you!" to the Sender of the box of suffering on your doorstep? In what ways can you start to be thankful for adversities?*

4. *When suffering, questions like, "Why me?" and "Why now?" are common. Why is God's question, "Why not?" important?*

5. *How do the sufferings of Job, Paul, Jesus, and others in Scripture help you in your walk of affliction? Give examples.*

But rejoice insofar as you share Christ's sufferings, that you may also rejoice and be glad when his glory is revealed. And after you have suffered a little while, the God of all grace, who has called you to his eternal glory in Christ, will himself restore, confirm, strengthen, and establish you.

1 Peter 4:13; 5:10

Behold, the dwelling place of God is with man.
He will dwell with them,
and they will be his people,
and God himself will be with them as their God.
He will wipe away every tear from their eyes,
and death shall be no more,
neither shall there be mourning,
nor crying, nor pain anymore,
for the former things have passed away.
Revelation 21:3-4

Looking Ahead

Change can be annoying for an older generation. We resist change as an unwanted and often unneeded challenge. It interrupts a familiar, predictable, and secure life. When change invades our private lives, upsetting comfortable routines, our complaints may roar loud enough for the rest of the world to know how we feel. Yet change is inevitable.

In our next Chapter, we will learn how God transforms our resistance to change into a gracious gift of aging.

It's Only Me

When we on Heaven's shores arrive,
One great consuming truth
Will be there waiting,
"It's only Me!"

Jesus, only Jesus, not you or me,
Will fill life, heart, and thought,
In me and in you,
A reflection of Him in us,
"It's only Me!"

Strange as strange may be,
Earthly thoughts may dimly be,
For that which occupy
Heaven's shores are only Him,
"It's only Me!"

No better time than now,
For heart and mind prepare,
When we arrive on Heaven's shores,
To see only Him,
"It's only Me!"

—Don Zoller, 2020

Change

Change is inevitable. It is pervasive. Yet our human nature resists it. Change comes hard with aging. It troubles and disturbs our security and comfort. In this Chapter, we will explore the impact of change on older people and discover what God says about change. How He transforms unwanted change into His gift of aging.

A Commitment to Change

I am not the person today I was yesterday,
Nor do I want to be the person tomorrow I am today.
Don Zoller

My Car and Change

I bought a car in 1972—my first *new* car. An Oldsmobile Delta 88. As I remember, it was a great car. A keeper! At least, that was what I thought at the time. A time when the lifespan of a car was short-lived.

With tender loving care, the car performed well for over twelve years. Then, it met its untimely demise in an accident. Totaled by a driver who ran a red light. Its final resting place was behind a secured ten-foot rust-infested wire fence protected by two very believable junkyard dogs. There the car sat, immovable—just a heap of twisted metal. Sad!

During those twelve years, the car met the needs of our growing family of five in reasonable comfort—as long as our youngest son remained in his car seat, and we didn't travel too far. Nana Jean, my wife's mother, was also a frequent passenger.

But as our family grew, even short distances became long and challenging. Later in the car's life, the family began to feel we were a bit like the TV series, *The Beverly Hillbillys* as we drove into the church parking lot on Sunday mornings. A parade of people dressed in their Sunday finest, emerging from a well-worn, visibly outdated car, caught the attention of other churchgoers. *It was quite a spectacle!*

As our children grew older, so did the car. It needed more tender, loving care. But I determined to keep it going. *No need to change to a newer car. This one works fine—most of the time!*

With frequent visits to the auto parts store and help from mechanics now and then, I managed to keep it running as our only car. My eldest son helped me install a new radiator. And I regularly poured cans of "please-help-me" additives into any opening in the engine I could find. Oil leaks and smell of gasoline was noticed.

Yes, the old car was aging, but it seemed to work fine if I didn't push it too hard. It was comfortable and familiar. I resisted the thought of buying a newer car. *Changing cars was unwanted and unneeded.*

I denied the obvious. As my car aged and became less reliable, change was now overdue. Yet, I resisted the thought. *Change seemed like a bad idea.* With the car's fatal accident, it was evident that God had something different in mind.

Something about our nature increasingly resists change, particularly as we age. As with my car, thoughts of change disturb our sense of what is familiar, secure, and important to us. How we feel about life—*how it used to be.* Bottomline: we don't like change. But like my car, life will someday end. Maybe abruptly. Change is inevitable, regardless of how much we resist it! But for us who are older, change can be a recurring challenge.

Truly, truly, I say to you, when you were young, you used to dress yourself and walk wherever you wanted, but when you are old, you will stretch out your hands, and another will dress you and carry you where you do not want to go. John 21:18

The Times, They Are Changing

By the time we're old, most of us have seen it all—well, almost all. Remarkable changes have paraded across the stage of our lives. Both good and bad.

People, places, and events have swarmed the corridors of our lives, demanding our attention and involvement. Many times, requiring us to change our thinking and behavior. Societal changes continually invade our lives. New technologies, ways of handling our money, novel medical procedures, ever-changing government regulations, and more.

Although good has come through change, many older people see change as unwanted and unnecessary. Digital kiosks to order fast food, multiple remotes to view TV. (Not long ago, we got up from our chair, walked across the room, and turned the knob to select the channels. Good exercise!); logins, passcodes, and passwords for everything else. Older people believe that few of these changes relate to their needs. They believe they are marginalized and not considered when changes occur. *We are expected to adapt.*

Older adults view their changing world as increasingly dangerous, chaotic, and uncertain. Simply, it's falling apart! However, each *departing generation* has always viewed their world as one step from falling off a cliff. King Solomon observed the truth about this view over three thousand years ago:

History merely repeats itself. It has all been done before. Nothing under the sun is truly new. Sometimes people say, "Here is something new!" But actually, it is old; nothing is ever truly new. We don't remember what happened in the past, and in future generations, no one will remember what we are doing now. Ecclesiastes 1:9–11, NLT

Throughout history, older generations typically resisted change. They saw little need for it. But there it was. On the horizon of their soon-to-be-harvested wheat field. A puff of black smoke. And with the black smoke came the unearthly noise of a horseless machine called a tractor. The older generation resisted. So many field workers would be out of work. Besides, this "tractor" thing frightened the farm animals and children. All running away. Hiding in fear. The tranquility of nature forever disturbed. What good was that! *This change was unacceptable! Unwanted and unneeded!*

From then on, the Industrial Revolution engulfed people near and far with puffs of black smoke and unearthly noises. A cascade of changes undermined a way of life held dear by many. An older generation saw such changes as wrong.

Since the beginning of the Industrial Revolution, changes have been vast, frequent, and overwhelming. From the telephone mounted on the wall to the iPhones we carry in our pockets or purses, changes abound.

As children, we were often on our own without our parents knowing exactly where we were or what we were doing—*all without a cell phone.* "Be home by supper" or "Be home before it gets dark" were the only instructions given. *Somehow, we lived to talk about it!*

Today, it's hard to imagine how someone could exist without an iPhone tucked away somewhere handy. *How things have changed!*

Using various social media, we talk to people worldwide, even people we do not know, and call them our "friends." Indeed, the older generation sees this change as a strange way to make friends.

In our generation, moving images came into our living rooms by a device called a television. At first (1920s), the screen size was about three inches when enlarged by a magnifying glass.[7] Today, it's, "How big a screen would you like?"

We were amazed to see men walk on the moon when a few years earlier, a flying machine barely got off the ground at Kitty Hawk. We buy things with plastic cards and write with pens that seem to go on forever without refilling from an inkwell. As you may remember, every school desk had inkwells and were kept filled religiously by the teacher. And cursive writing? Seemingly, a lost art form.

We now send messages from a computer or text from our phones rather than paper and pen. Of course, there is no postage required. That saves money! Changes in medicine and medical care border on the miraculous.

The internet has opened an almost infinite wealth of knowledge. College degrees are possible to earn while going no further than across the room to our computer. All our questions answered! Answered in an instant. Three-dimensional printing allows a computer to build almost anything (even my crown for a tooth while I waited). With the arrival of artificial intelligence (AI), thinking has become optional. There is more to come. It will come fast! Change!

Thousands of life-changing innovations have occurred in our lifetime. Most have greatly impacted our lives. Many are beyond our capacity to understand. Yes. Some have caused us to cringe and recoil.

Too Close to Home

Some changes can disturb the personal lives of older adults. These changes edge too close to home, affecting our routines and habits. Displeasure is quickly expressed when comfort and safety are threatened. *"We are not happy campers!"*

How the older generation experiences church worship is one example. Many remember a predictable, familiar, and comfortable form of traditional worship— a form of worship our parents remembered from their childhood. Hymn books, choir, organ, and pews.

However, this predictable, dignified traditional worship has disappeared from most churches today. Replaced mainly by a "loud performance" of contemporary praise music. For many who are older, such music is highly repetitious, unfamiliar, and noisy. It is difficult for them to sing, thus, to worship. Hymn books, choir, and organ have disappeared from many churches, along with the pews. In fact, the traditional Sunday School—a favorite among seniors—is sometimes hard to find.

Many, including the pastor, dress casually, with only older men wearing coats and ties. Neither do church-attending women adorn their heads with floral hats. Wearing one's "Sunday's finest" is obsolete! *Why can't we just worship the way we used to?*

Older adults do not trust what they do not understand and cannot see or touch. Changes in modern-day banking and purchasing causes an older generation to vent their mistrust and concerns. The banking industry discourages the use of checks and cash. Soon, paper currency will no longer be used or accepted in many places. With the increase of electronic payments and transfers as the preferred way to do banking, older adults are stranded on an island of uncertainty and confusion. Such confusion fosters potential for financial fraud and deception.

There was a time when going to the bank was commonplace. A frequent community happening. We presented our bank book to the teller to record our deposits and withdrawals. Banks, a place of exchange and commerce, where people waited in long lines to do their banking (no one seemed to be in a hurry), today are empty. Tellers may be hard to find but are still available—for older people. Most banks prefer for customers to use "drive-thru" or online computer banking. Such encounters feel impersonal and unfriendly for older people. In their day, doing business was casual, concluded amenably by word of mouth or a handshake. *Times have changed!*

Many older adults prefer to pay with cash or write checks at the grocery store. They pay their bills by writing checks from their kitchen table, concluding the transaction by putting a stamp on the envelope for mailing, or going to a local store to pay the utility bill.

Forget the bank's computer-generated statement. They want the ability to balance their checkbooks (something a younger generation knows little about) against a monthly statement the bank sends them in the mail, not by email—*it's what they are used to!* To have someone automatically withdraw money from their bank account is a change too far! *Why can't I write checks or pay with cash like I used to?*

Our ability to taste certain foods and maintain an appetite may be a problem as we age. Our minds remember a specific taste, but it's gone when we bite into our favorite food. Perhaps a new cook in the kitchen has no idea what this should taste like. Maybe it's a new recipe with different ingredients? *Why can't they make it the way it has always been made?*

However, more than likely, the problem is with us. Our taste buds change as we age, making food taste different and less appealing. Sometimes, with little taste at all. Appetites diminish. *So much for the pumpkin pie that Mother used to make.*

Whatever happened to family dinner time—a time around the table to be together, talk, and enjoy a good hot meal? How quaint! In many homes today, it's "grab and go." The dining room episodes from *Father Knows Best* or *Leave It to Beaver* are remembered no more. We who are older look on with horror. *What's a dining room? Nothing is quite the same as it used to be! Change!*

We resist change in so many different areas of our lives. Perhaps the most obvious way we resist change—the one closest to home—is how we look in the mirror!

Mirror, Mirror on the Wall . . .

Our mirror daily records the unforgiving and irreversible change of a body that is decaying *(Genesis 3:19)*. Life's big challenge is accepting and embracing our changing image with peace and grace. A gift God has given us to enjoy.

God allows change to touch our lives through world events, relationships with others, and our deteriorating bodies. But change is not the problem. It's how we deal with change that becomes a problem.

Resisting change we see in our mirror puts us at cross purpose with God's order in His creation. God uses change to keep our tent pegs loose and prepare us for our eternal home. The more we remain flexible, the more we will experience His eternal purpose for us. One day, we will be like Him. *The most remarkable change of all!*

Let's consider how God views change and makes change into a gift of aging.

The God Who Doesn't Change

Scripture reminds us that God is consistently the same *"yesterday, today, and forever" (Hebrew 13:8)*. He never changes. Yet He commands and executes change continuously throughout His created universe. With awe and wonder, we observe these changes through telescopes in space to the most sophisticated microscopes—all beyond the unaided eye. Everything is in motion and constantly changing from the furthest galaxies to the smallest particles in our bodies.

Change surrounds us. What we were yesterday is not what we are today. The dust in our homes is partly who we were yesterday! Discarded cells from our skin are shed and become the dust we see. Our bodies constantly shed and replace cells. An exciting account of how our bodies continue to change—made new—through human cell replacement is found in a short article in Appendix 4, page 213.

The process of change is one way God manages what He created for the praise of His glory. Even our relationship with Christ requires us to change:

"But grow in the grace and knowledge of our Lord and Savior Jesus Christ" 2 Peter 3:18.

Nana Jean, my wife's mother, eagerly welcomed change. She embraced the latest innovations. At 102 years old, she learned how to operate the Apple iPad. Remaining flexible, curious, and passionate about life allowed her to change and adapt to life around her graciously. Her attitude toward change can benefit all of us who are in the Autumn of Life.

Dealing With Unwanted Change

Change is inevitable, yet often unwanted. But change can serve God's purpose when it contributes to our good.

The best way to deal with these changes is to recognize and accept them with grace and thanksgiving as part of God's created order. Then submit what you resist to God. Let Him do what He does best—transforms the unwanted into a gift of aging. This can be done by focusing and anchoring our hearts on the One who never changes.

Changes will come our way as we walk with Jesus. How we respond measures our progress in becoming more like Him. Jesus hated the cross. He despised the shame and torture of what that cross met. He wanted this event removed. But in the garden, Jesus surrendered this unwanted experience to His Father—*"Not my will, but yours be done."* We further read,

*"With joy, He endured the cross for what lies ahead."
(Hebrews 12:2)*

The first step for dealing with unwanted change is surrendering our spirit of resistance. If our focus is on Jesus and His glory in old age, the little things that disturb us become opportunities to "enter the garden of surrender" with Jesus. Here, we will be *transformed by the renewal of your mind, that by testing you may discern what is the good and acceptable and perfect will of God"* (Romans 12:2). After all, isn't that what we really want to do at this point in our lives?

The second step is to give thanks. If change comes as something different from how we used to do things, ask God to transform it into a gift. He designed change to produce thanksgiving and to draw our hearts to Christ. It is His gift of grace and mercy intended to bless us. God loves us. He wants nothing to diminish our relationship with Him. Not even our attitude toward change.

Giving thanks always and for everything to God the Father in the name of our Lord Jesus Christ. Ephesians 5:20, emphasis added

Rejoice always, pray without ceasing, give thanks in all circumstances; for this is the will of God in Christ Jesus for you. Do not quench the Spirit. 1 Thessalonians 5:16–19, emphasis added

The third step is to be joyful. Joy follows thanksgiving as we surrender our resistance to unwanted change. We should be joyfully delighted that God is busy in our lives! God wants the joy of a resurrected Jesus to be ours, *"These things have I spoken to you, that my joy may be in you, and that your joy may be full" (John 15:11).*

The God who does not change is continually at work in us to bring about change to our lives—bringing us to surrender, thanksgiving, and joy.

Neither retirement nor old age exempts us from spiritual change. Our daily walk with Jesus will produce change as we become more like Him in thought, word, and deed in our older years. Let's be thankful and joyful that unwanted change can be transformed into a gift of aging!

One caveat about change. When change requires we act counter to the teaching of Scripture, when change challenges the character of God and His glory, we need to say, "No!" Be resolute and faithful to the King of Glory. Biblical wisdom is essential when confronted with questionable change.

The Book of Daniel provides an example of a change that contradicted God's glory. A command was given to ensure loyalty, requiring everyone in Babylon to bow down and worship the king's golden statue.

This command included three young Hebrew men. They knew worshiping this idol would dishonor the God whom they served. Here is their response to this unwanted change—a change ordered by government decree:

Shadrach, Meshach, and Abednego replied, "O Nebuchadnezzar, we do not need to defend ourselves before you.

If we are thrown into the blazing furnace, the God whom we serve is able to save us. He will rescue us from your power, Your Majesty.

But even if he doesn't, we want to make it clear to you, Your Majesty, that we will never serve your gods or worship the gold statue you have set up. Daniel 3:16–18, NLT

God calls us to become imitators of His changeless grace, mercy, and peace as we walk through life with Him. We are to reflect His eternal unchanging love to a world of constant change. A world submerged in darkness and self-deceit. He alone is the anchor and steadfast hope in a sea of change and decay.

But for us, our challenge requires giving up resistance to change and submit to His Spirit. The One who teaches us to be thankful for all things (even when facing unwanted changes) and to rejoice always. This is God's gift of aging!

Let's Talk About It

1. *How is change a problem for you? In what ways do you resist change?*

2. *How does getting older affect your willingness to accept change?*

3. *Why does God, who is unchanging, expect us to change?*

4. *How would you transform an unwanted change into a Gift from God, i.e., The Gift of Change?*

5. *How is being flexible, curious, and passionate about life important as we grow older?*

6. *In what ways are surrender, thanksgiving, and joy critical to change?*

And we all, with unveiled face, beholding the glory of the Lord, are being transformed into the same image from one degree of glory to another. For this comes from the Lord who is the Spirit. 2 Corinthians 3:18

The More We Know God

The more we know God
The more we will know ourselves.
The more we know God,
The more will we understand our past.
The more we know God,
The more we will focus on what is eternal.

—*Don Zoller, 2003*

Looking Ahead

Most of us are keenly aware of limitations that afflict us as we age. Physical, mental, and perhaps emotional limitations confront and often frustrate us. But it is difficult to imagine our limitations as a gift.

In our next Chapter, we will discover how limitations help accomplish God's purpose for our lives. Because of His amazing grace, limitations that overwhelm us can be transformed into His gift of aging.

On Growing Old—Or Is It Just Older

We still see the beauty of flowers in bloom,

We still hear the birds,

A chorus of heavenly music

We still feel the touch of a loving hand

From a friend drawing close.

These, and so much more.

We are not old, just older.

Although pieces are coming unglued,

We are aging toward perfection.

—Don Zoller, 2018
Psalm 92:12–15

Limitations

When we think of limitations as older adults, we often picture canes, walkers, wheelchairs, and broken bodies. We may not drive at night or travel far from home. However, a more common limitation is self-imposed, "I'm just too old."

God uses the challenge of our limitations as an opportunity to display His presence in our lives. He uses weak and broken vessels to advance the work of His kingdom. We will see how He is sufficient in our weakness to accomplish more than we could ever imagine. Come along and see how God uses limitations in amazing ways.

Limitations Abound

L imitations come with aging. Most of us can no longer jump out of airplanes, climb ladders, or even dance the boogie-woogie. We walk slower. Our gait is not as energetic or confident. Physical and mental limitations eventually creep into our once-robust lives.

Limitations come in all shapes and sizes, each begging for attention. As we age, bones, muscles, and nerves heal more slowly. Recovery from a fall or surgery may require a cane, walker, or wheelchair to remain mobile. Limitations curtail a once-active lifestyle. We may see ourselves as "laid aside," unable to achieve any meaningful purpose in life.

Reoccurring aches and pains may hinder our involvement in physical activity. Digestive issues often govern what and how much we eat. Casual conversations become opportunities for hearing difficulties that marginalize our ability to engage with others. Painful hips, knees, and backs challenge simple walking or sitting. And afternoon naps? They seem to be a necessity rather than a preference. Our vision diminishes. *Now, where did I put my glasses?*

"I am just too old" is a frequent self-imposed limitation. Many older adults have adopted this limitation to excuse themselves from living life to its fullest within the boundaries of their physical or mental condition. Admittedly, life is harder with disabilities— much harder! But we are still breathing, and we still wake up on the green side of the grass. Excusing ourselves because of our limitations and turning inward is not where we want to be in our senior years. Remember Myrna (Chapter 3). How have others handled their limitations? Let's find out.

Overcoming Our limitations

When sin entered the human experience, so did limitations of body and mind. However, when we view the panorama of history, we see many who have faced the challenges of their limitations and yet remained productive:

Ludwig van Beethoven, born in 1770, a prolific German classical music composer and pianist. Hundreds of musical masterpieces, including Symphony Five and Symphony Nine, being among his most outstanding, have endured the ages. However, Beethoven was completely deaf when he composed most of his significant work. *(Wikipedia)*

Helen Adams Keller, born in 1880, contracted an illness that left her deaf and blind at the early age of nineteen months. As an author, political activist, lecturer, and disability rights advocate, her writings included fourteen books and hundreds of essays, and she gave many speeches on various topics. Keller attended Harvard and became the first deafblind person in the United States to earn a Bachelor of Arts degree. She worked for the American Foundation for the Blind (AFB), traveling to thirty-five countries advocating for those with vision loss until she died in 1968. *(Wikipedia)*

Franklin Delano Roosevelt, born in 1882, served as the thirty-second president of the United States during the demanding years of the Great Depression and World War II. Before becoming president in 1932, Roosevelt contracted polio, which permanently paralyzed his legs. Until he died in 1945, he performed his duties as president confined to a wheelchair. *(Wikipedia)*

Stephen William Hawking, born in 1942, was a theoretical physicist, cosmologist, and author. He was the research director at the Center for Theoretical Cosmology at the University of Cambridge. Severely disabled in body and speech, Hawking was confined to a wheelchair. He died in 2018 at the age of 76 after having motor neuron disease (MND) for more than fifty years. *(Wikipedia)*

Andrea Bocelli, an Italian tenor, was born visually impaired with congenital glaucoma. When he was twelve, Bocelli became completely blind following a brain hemorrhage resulting from an accident. He developed his singing career and became an internationally acclaimed classical and pop singer. Bocelli has received a cascade of awards and prestigious acclaim as having one of the most beautiful male voices in the world. *(Wikipedia)*

Joni Eareckson Tada, born in 1949, a Christian author, radio host, artist, and founder of Joni and Friends, a Christian ministry to the disability community. Tada is the author of over forty-eight books about disability and Christianity. At the age of seventeen, she became quadriplegic as a result of a diving accident in shallow water. She has been confined to her wheelchair for over fifty-five years while serving her Lord. *(Wikipedia)*

Nicholas Vujicic, born in 1982, an Australian-American Christian evangelist and motivational speaker. Vujicic travels internationally and speaks about his testimony of faith in Jesus Christ. He is a graduate of Griffith University, Australia. Married with four children, and founded ministry organizations, including "Champions for the Brokenhearted" and "Life Without Limbs." Vujicic was born with tetra-amella syndrome—without arms or legs. Using a stylus in his mouth, he types forty-three words a minute on his computer and continues to serve God while seeing the ministry grow. *(Wikipedia)*

Consider the Scriptures

The Scriptures provide examples of how God used people with limitations and disabilities to further His kingdom.

Moses had an unknown speech impediment *(Exodus 4:10)* and needed Aaron to speak for him before Pharoah. Yet God used Moses, an eighty-year-old man, to lead over two million Israelites out of Egypt through the wilderness for forty years. There, he met with God, lived to talk about it, and declared The Ten Commandments still in use today *(Deuteronomy 34:5–12)*. *God blessed him!*

Then there was *Caleb*. As an old man of eighty-five years, he refused the excuse that he was too old for the rigors of warfare. Instead, he insisted on engaging in battle, taking back from the enemy the land belonging to Israel *(Numbers 14:24)*. *God blessed him.*

Jacob acquired a family inheritance by deception, alienated his brother, brought grief to his father, and served his uncle in bondage for twenty-two years. Then, God met Jacob in a special way. Jacob wrestled with God—for a whole night. Finally, God touched him, dislocating his hip. In pain, he leaned on his cane for the rest of his life. A limitation given to him by God, but God also gave Jacob a new life and a new name—Israel *(Genesis 19:24–32)*. He became the father of the twelve tribes of Israel. To this day, there is a land and a people after his name. *God blessed him.*

The *Apostle Paul* endured a body marked with permanent bruises and scars from the torture of multiple imprisonments, beatings, shipwrecks, and thieves *(2 Corinthians 11:23–29)*. As if those afflictions were not enough, the Lord allowed Paul to endure a persistent and severe pain that greatly weakened his body *(2 Corinthians 12:7–10)*. We do not know precisely what Paul's physical limitation was, but we do know he stayed true to his mission *(Acts 9:15–16) (2 Timothy 4:6–8)*. *God blessed him!*

Timothy, a disciple and spiritual son of the aging Apostle Paul, pastored the Church at Ephesus. There, Timothy faced many challenges with a new church—proper worship, ensuring the appointment of godly leadership, dealing with false teachers, and guarding relationships within the church. Paul, from prison, also asked him to make the arduous trip to Rome to see him. But Timothy was not a healthy man. He suffered from a long-term intestinal illness but remained a faithful servant of the Lord *(1 Timothy 5:23)*. *God blessed him!*

Throughout church history, many servants of God have been limited physically yet remained faithful unto death. With a deep sense of mission that overshadowed their physical disabilities, they pressed on to achieve a greater reward than this life had to offer—*of whom the world was not worthy:* ·

Well done, good and faithful servant. You have been faithful over a little; I will set you over much. Enter into the joy of your master. Matthew 25:21

These are but a few, both past and present, who with their limitations, show us the possibility of a productive life. Yes. They all struggled at the beginning of their arduous journey and continued to struggle throughout their lives. But with great sacrifice, hardship, and pain they offered their God-given gifts and abilities to benefit others.

In many cases, their determination advanced God's kingdom to demonstrate His power infused in yielded clay vessels no matter their condition. The vessel may be cracked, chipped, or broken, but the presence of God's power in that vessel makes the difference. For this reason, any old vessel will do to display His life-changing power *(Exodus 3:2)*.

As you face your limitations, remember He has chosen you regardless of your condition to serve Him. He has set before you unimaginable opportunities to advance His kingdom. Even in small ways. When God occupies a cracked or broken vessel, nothing is small or without possibilities.

* * * *

Who Are We?

Our disabilities or limitations do not define us. Such inconveniences and obstacles are only outward adornments God gives us to achieve a unique and uncommon work for His kingdom. A task that will one day be revealed for the praise of His glory. Therefore, in the face of our limitations, remain flexible, curious, and passionate about life. Beneath the skin of broken bodies, we are those who God designed us to be—the person we truly are!

So we do not lose heart. Though our outer self is wasting away, our inner self is being renewed day by day. For this light momentary affliction is preparing for us an eternal weight of glory beyond all comparison, as we look not to the things that are seen but to the things that are unseen. For the things that are seen are transient, but the things that are unseen are eternal. 2 Corinthians 4:16–18

At eighty-eight years old, I experience the expected pains and aches shared by most my age. Most aches and pains are a nuisance and non-limiting. However, there are a few that are more problematic. A detached retina left me with distorted vision that is helped by a corrective prescription. A minor limitation. A broken femur bone married me to my cane—a minor limitation. Two years ago, I was diagnosed with congestive heart failure. This condition could result in instant death. This, too, a minor limitation. My departure time is in God's hands. It's true for all of us.

In these later years, God has inspired me to write, and I trust for His glory. I keep going, never knowing if I will be around to finish the following sentence. And that's okay. My immediate goal is to maintain a focus that is onward and upward. Such a goal is something each of us can pursue regardless of our limitations or disability.

God has gifted us with the ability to bless others to bring glory to Him. Let's let our gifts shine through our limitations and disabilities. Not bury them by dwelling on our circumstances. Let's not look inward and feel sorry for ourselves. Learn to look upward to an Almighty God, not for healing, but for purpose. Look outward and ask how we can bless someone today with kindness and a word of encouragement! Something our divided world desperately needs.

Our attitude can change toward our disabilities and limitations. God can transform our challenges from a consuming burden to a gift of aging. He can do this immediately or over time to deepen our faith and trust in Him. His passion is to change us into someone new.

We may see ourselves as a *Mephibosheth*, lame in both feet from an early age. Disabled. Limited. But be encouraged. We are forever richly blessed by the King. To sit with Him at His table *(2 Samuel 4:4; Chapter 9)*. God's gift of aging.

"God loves to make possible what the world considers impossible, and He loves to use powerfully those the world considers incapable." Megan Cornwell, February 23, 2023, Christianity Magazine

But I will sing of your strength,

in the morning I will sing of your love;

for you are my fortress,

my refuge in times of trouble.

You are my strength, I sing praise to you;

you, God, are my fortress,

my God on whom I can rely.

Psalm 59:16–17

New International Version

Let's Talk About It

1. How do you deal with your limitations? In what ways do they restrict your life and activities?

2. From the list of those who have overcome the challenges of their limitations and disabilities (Pages 101–105), who do you know that could be added to the list? What has been the impact of their lives on yours?

3. In what ways can God use you to advance His kingdom work despite your limitations or disabilities?

4. What changes are needed in your life for God to transform your limitations into a gift of aging?

For He knows how we are formed; He remembers that we are dust. Psalm 103:14

My flesh and my heart may fail, but God is the strength of my heart and my portion forever. Psalm 73:26

Looking Ahead

Being smart is not the same as being wise. Being smart measures what we know. Being wise is how well we use what we know. The Bible defines smart as the wisdom of this world when such knowledge presumes upon those things that are eternal. God calls it foolishness *1 Corinthians 5:19*. Human intellect cannot find or define God.

The next Chapter will help us understand true wisdom. God's protective shield for older adults. We will see how God adorns our years with His wisdom. And how His wisdom becomes His gift of aging.

God moves in a mysterious way
His wonders to perform
He plants His footsteps in the sea
and rides upon the storm.
Deep in unsearchable mines
of never-failing skill
He treasures up His bright designs
and works His sovereign will.

by William Cowper, 1773
Public Domain

Wisdom

Wisdom is something many people wish for. Life is hard, but to have wisdom would undoubtedly help in making important life decisions. It provides the roadmap to navigate the uncharted and uncertain landscape of life. Wisdom becomes the anchor so often needed as we age.

Many exert a lot of effort to acquire human knowledge. Few seek wisdom — true wisdom. The distinction between the two is often confused. Yet to know the difference is essential in the Autumn of Life.

In this Chapter, we will discover the Fountain and the Giver of Wisdom. But as we begin our search, we will find wisdom in a very unlikely place.

In Search of Wisdom

C ome with me. Let's discover wisdom. Walk with me down dimly lit aisles of ancient libraries filled with volumes of dusty books. Undisturbed by time. Ageless books that hold the wisdom of philosophers who chronicle the depths of human experience. A flood of ponderous words overwhelms our long but fruitless search. Words of human reason abound telling us how best to live in our present world, but nothing of eternal value. Searching the aisles of antiquity for wisdom comes to an end. Hoping for a wisdom they do not have. Only emptiness and darkness remain.

Now, let's walk the austere halls of academic learning. Hopefully, we may acquire knowledge that leads to wisdom. We learn about how the universe was made, how people behave, and how information is processed. We learn how things work but not the wisdom that causes things to be or why they exist. Alas, we end our pursuit of wisdom as we began. Empty.

Or we may venture to distant lands to seek out monks, priests, and sages. They have meditated deeply about life. Surely, we can glean from them the wisdom we seek. For such wisdom, we endure the rigors of climbing unwelcoming and precipitous mountains. But return disappointed. Our effort is in vain. Many words of moral beauty but no true wisdom. Nothing to refresh and enrich a parched soul moving toward an eternal destiny. Only emptiness and darkness.

Although we have touched the pinnacle of wisdom, it is only the wisdom of this world. Such wisdom can never satisfy the ache residing in the human heart. God tells us why:

For the wisdom of this world is folly with God. For it is written, "He catches the wise in their craftiness," and again, "The Lord knows the thoughts of the wise, that they are futile." 1 Corinthians 3:19–20

We long for eternal, timeless, life-changing wisdom that God alone provides. Come with me where few venture to find wisdom. An unlikely place indeed.

A Walk Through the Cemetery

A cemetery. We approach the open gates to this place of final rest. The message is obvious. A message that frames the beginning of our journey in search for wisdom: *That which is born, dies. There is a time for both.*

For everything there is a season, and a time for every matter under heaven: a time to be born, and a time to die . . .
Ecclesiastes 3:1–2

Since his days are determined, and the number of his months is with you, and you have appointed his limits that he cannot pass. Job 14:5

Scanning the neatly manicured grass, our view is soon interrupted. What immediately captures the eye are headstones. Lots of them. Some upright. Others lie flat on the ground. Grass, and sometimes weeds may invade the inscriptions. Headstones tell us where the remains of people are buried.

As we come closer, we notice each headstone is etched with a unique inscription. A concise history of a person who used to be but is no more. Maybe there is a caption, "In Loving Memory," which is always nice to see. The name of the person on the headstone captures our interest. Sometimes, we see their relationship to the family. Then there are a couple of dates. When the person was born and when they died. Two events separated by *a dash*. The span of an earthly life compressed into a simple dash between two dates.

Let's stop here. Think about the meaning of that little dash. Contained in that little mark, a dash between the two dates, is the summation of life. Someday, the entirety of our lives will be represented by just a simple, unadorned dash. *Isn't that exciting?*

Think about what this dash means. Every breath we took, every thought we had, every spoken word, all engraved within this little dash. Yes. Everything we did and everything we were. It's all here in that short little dash between two dates.

With each passing generation our life story contained in that dash fades. The meaning of this small, insignificant mark is gradually forgotten. Without fanfare or ceremony, what is remembered soon passes. This dash—our life— is remembered by only a very few. Finally, they, too, will pass away. All will be forgotten. The Apostle James says it clearly enough:

What is your life? For you are a mist that appears for a little time and then vanishes. James 4:14

Our search for God's wisdom begins with understanding and accepting the brevity of life. On the stage of human history, our short lives, accomplishments, adulations, hopes, and dreams mean little in view of eternity—fleeting like the morning mist. A dash that fades and is remembered no more.

Human wisdom tells us that everything about our dash will evaporate into nothingness. Only the present exists. And like the morning mist, the meaning of life becomes questionable and without lasting purpose. The conclusion of worldly wisdom is nihilism— nothingness. No. *This won't do!*

O Lord, make me know my end and what is the measure of my days; let me know how fleeting I am! Behold, you have made my days a few handbreadths, and my lifetime is as nothing before you. Surely all mankind stands as a mere breath! Selah   *Psalm 39:4–5*

The setting of *James 4:13–15* shows us the next step to discover wisdom. God is sovereign. He has a say in everything there is. Even those things contained within our dash. He alone extends our dash into eternity and makes it a lifeline without end. He alone gives purpose and meaning to life. He alone, not human wisdom, determines true significance and value to life *(Romans 8:37–39)*.

God's Wisdom, A Breath Away

We don't need to visit ancient libraries and halls of academic learning or climb distant mountains to find enduring wisdom. Wisdom is right at hand:

> *For this commandment that I command you today is not too hard for you, neither is it far off. It is not in heaven, that you should say, 'Who will ascend to heaven for us and bring it to us, that we may hear it and do it?' Neither is it beyond the sea, that you should say, 'Who will go over the sea for us and bring it to us, that we may hear it and do it?' But the word is very near you. It is in your mouth and in your heart, so that you can do it. Deuteronomy 30:11–14, emphasis added*

Wisdom is but a breath away. Just ask God, who generously gives wisdom. Ask in faith, believing He will respond to our request. When we receive God's wisdom and put it to use, He gets the glory. This is always a good thing.

If any of you lacks wisdom, let him ask God, who gives generously to all without reproach, and it will be given him. But let him ask in faith, with no doubting, for the one who doubts is like a wave of the sea that is driven and tossed by the wind. James 1:5–7, emphasis added

. . . that the God of our Lord Jesus Christ, the Father of glory, may give you the Spirit of wisdom and of revelation in the knowledge of him, having the eyes of your hearts enlightened, that you may know what is the hope to which he has called you . Ephesians 1:17–18, emphasis added

Whatever you ask in my name, this I will do, that the Father may be glorified in the Son. If you ask me anything in my name, I will do it. John 14:13–14

Go ahead. Ask God for the wisdom you need as an older person to navigate life's unchartered and uncertain paths. Just a simple believing request is all you need.

Practical Wisdom for Living

Biblical wisdom is not another philosophical view of life to embrace. It is not one among many from which to choose. No. God's wisdom is uniquely different. Set apart from all other forms of earthbound wisdom, God's wisdom cannot co-exist with any other forms of wisdom. Learn to embrace His wisdom fully!

Ephesians 1:17–22 explains that God's wisdom is infused by the Holy Spirit. Energized by the Spirit, this wisdom transforms our spiritual insight so we can know the heart and purpose of God. It provides understanding of God's view of the world. In fact, our very lives. It imparts knowledge of the eternal God in whom our life is secure in Christ. Bottom line, such wisdom is transformative. It changes who we are, how we think, and how we behave. It guides us in our daily lives.

Scripture is bathed with divine wisdom. It's all there! Just look for it *(John 5:39)*. But seek wisdom with a receptive heart and a commitment to apply it. Only then will we become wise with God's wisdom:

My child, listen to what I say, and treasure my commands. Tune your ears to wisdom and concentrate on understanding. Cry out for insight and ask for understanding. Search for them as you would for silver; seek them like hidden treasures. Then you will understand what it means to fear the LORD, and you will gain knowledge of God. For the LORD grants wisdom! From his mouth come knowledge and understanding. He grants a treasure of common sense to the honest. He is a shield to those who walk with integrity. He guards the paths of the just and protects those who are faithful to him. Then you will understand what is right, just, and fair, and you will find the right way to go. For wisdom will enter your heart, and knowledge will fill you with joy. Wise choices will watch over you. Understanding will keep you safe. Proverbs 2:1-11, NLT

Wisdom tells us who God is and who we are. God is neither our buddy nor the person behind the window at the drive-thru bank doling out what we ask for. We ask for wisdom on God's terms, not ours. He is God, and we are not. He created the universe and all that it contains. He is enthroned in unapproachable light. Immortal. He is sovereign and ruler of all *(1 Timothy 6:15–16)*.

We are His *dust* creatures. Blown and scattered by winds of uncertainty. Temporal. As we approach an awesome and holy God, creator, and sustainer of all things, a reverential fear should frame our posture. Utter humbleness. With a deep sense of awe of His presence we begin the journey toward wisdom. With godly fear, awe, and humility, we discover who God is. We are now ready for the next step *(Proverbs 2:5; 1 Peter 5:6)*.

Invited by God Himself, we are free to ask for wisdom who generously give it without rebuke or shame *(James 1:5)*. It is given out of His eternal love for us in Christ. God longs to fill us with the knowledge of Himself and the plans He has for our lives.

But wisdom is not a bag of freebies. Wisdom must be learned, often through rough and tumble life experiences. In *James 3:13–18*, we recognize wisdom not only by what it looks like but also how it behaves. We learn wisdom in the school of humility and meekness. James M Barrie says it well, *"Life is a long lesson in humility."*[8]

An ancient rabbinical teaching says, *"If you don't do it, you don't know it!"* From a biblical perspective, wisdom that is not applied to life is meaningless.

. . . for my people have committed two evils: they have forsaken me, the fountain of living waters, and hewed out cisterns for themselves, broken cisterns that can hold no water. Jeremiah 2:13

Stumbling around in the dark is no fun for older people. Especially when trying to figure out which direction to go or make decisions in a chaotic world. The decisions and uncertainties of life make God's wisdom a necessity.

Concluding Thoughts

Learning godly wisdom is a daily response to God's word. Wisdom abounds within its pages. Seek His face continually. Learn His ways. Wisdom will guard our thoughts and ways. God's wisdom protects us against the evil subtleties of this world. Not only does it bring us to salvation *(2 Timothy 3:15)*, wisdom ushers us into a wholesome alignment with the mind of God.

Wisdom gained from God's Word becomes a life-giving resource when His Spirit calls us to help others along this journey of life. Many aging people need

God's wisdom. The wisdom God gives us may be what they need.

The Lord God has given me the tongue of those who are taught, that I may know how to sustain with a word him who is weary. Morning by morning he awakens, he awakens my ear to hear as those who are taught. Isaiah 50:4

Let's allow the challenge of uncertainties move us to ask for this joyful and gracious gift of wisdom—His gift of aging.

Let's Talk About It

1. *Discuss the difference between "worldly wisdom" and God's Wisdom. Give examples of worldly wisdom, i.e., street wisdom that influences your life.*

2. *What ideas in this Chapter were most meaningful for you? How did they apply to your life?*

3. *When you think of wisdom, which specific part is your greatest need. How can you trust God to meet that need?*

4. *From the Scripture verses cited in the Chapter, which affected you the most? How does it influence your thinking and behavior?*

Beloved, we are God's children now, and what we will be, has not yet appeared; but we know that when he appears we shall be like him, because we shall see him as he is. And everyone who thus hopes in him purifies himself as he is pure.

1 John 3:2–3

Looking Ahead

Older adults need relationships that abide and go deep. From the moment of our birth, God's creative plan is for relationships. We were not meant to live alone. After all, *"It is not good that man (or woman) should be alone"* *(Genesis 2:18, emphasis added)*.

Yet many relationships have been disfigured due to our human condition—sin. Relationships become twisted and broken. Heartache, depression, and loneliness result. Even death separates loved ones.

In the next Chapter, let's find out how God uses the challenge of relationships to transform them into a gift of aging.

So even to old age and gray hairs,

O God, do not forsake me,

until I proclaim your might to another generation,

your power to all those to come.

Psalm 71:18

7

Relationships

Life is about relationships. From a nursing infant held closely to its mother to those who are aging—bed-bound, barely speaking, relationships are indispensable. That's the way God planned it. Being alone, truly alone, is never how God intended it to be. "It is not good that man (or woman) should be alone" Genesis 2:18, emphasis added. Yet, in our busy world of instant communication, social acquaintances often masquerade as relationships. Arranged to meet a specific need for a moment in time, many acquaintances are fleeting and shallow. Positive, productive relationships are essential for senior adults. Relationships that abide and go deep. Come, let's see how God uses the challenge of relationships to transform them into true friends as His gift to us.

Problem Relationships

R elationships can be beautiful. Wonderful expressions of togetherness, bonding, with the warmth of human touch. The fountain of intimacy and an anchor for the soul in times of stress and uncertainty. Often, a lifeline of encouragement. A blessing!

But we know the sad reality. Relationships aren't perfect! We would like them to be, but it isn't necessarily the way they are. In fact, relationships within families can be dysfunctional. Healthy relationships so often are in short supply. Relationships can be shredded, twisted, and broken through harm or neglect. Unhappily, in our senior years, broken relationships often bring heartache, depression, and loneliness.

Problem relationships become *deficit* relationships. Falling short of attachment and intimacy. Dutiful. Perfunctory. Infrequent and superficial contact with family and friends can leave a painful gap in the experience of an older adult, especially when they live alone.

Family Relationships

Relationships between older adults and their families can be a challenge. Differences in lifestyles, interests, personalities, and finances are often sources of irritation and conflict. How these differences are managed vary depending on the family's ability and commitment to accommodate their aging member.

The Intuits[9], a native Arctic tribe, had a custom of how best to accommodate their elderly. An aging member who could no longer contribute to the family's well-being was placed on a small ice floe—*heading south.*

The family led their elderly member to a temporary home—an ice floe—among the frigid waters of the north. With provisions to last a week: a blanket, a few personal belongings, and appropriate prayers, they placed their loved one comfortably on the ice floe and said their goodbyes. In the face of dire resources this solution meant the survival of the family. Everyone agreed. Even its oldest member.

Although the ice floe solution was an accepted custom for the Intuits at the time, it is no longer practiced. But, in our culture today, aging members can be abandoned to an "ice floe" by their families for various reasons. These reasons may be financial, social, or practical considerations, even convenience. But the result is usually the same. The aging member is alone.

Yes. Families can neglect their aging members, especially those in their own homes. Busy lives and forgetfulness often result in neglected and lonely seniors. Being lonely is real, and it affects many older people. Those that seek meaningful relationships with their families but come up empty.

But putting an aging family member on an ice floe is not the only option. Many families have provided wonderfully for their senior members by making living arrangements that are supportive, intimate, and caring, with frequent contact by family and friends. *All good!*

Nana Jean and Our Family

In the formative years of our marriage, Grandpa and Grandma always lived close to our family—within a few blocks of us. Our relationship was positive and productive. When Grandpa died, Nana Jean, my wife's mother, continued to live nearby in her own home. Being nearby allowed for frequent visits by our family. Going to Nana's house for chocolate chip cookies after school was always a treat enjoyed by our three sons.

When Nana Jean graduated into her eighties, we agreed she would be welcomed as part of our family— under one roof. We invited Nana Jean to pull up her tent pegs and come live with us as a *together* family.

Adjusting to Nana Jean living in our home was not difficult. She was ready. So were we. She came not as storage or an *extra suitcase* but *as an essential member* of the family.

We made sure she had everything she needed to be comfortable. Always the master bedroom suite. An extra sitting room and free access to the house. She went where we went. Helped in the kitchen, cared for her part of the house, and more. Our home was her home. Completely!

Although she engaged freely with the family, she instinctively knew when it was time for her to retire to her sitting room and allow the family to enjoy their private time.

Joining our family of five became a blessing. Nana Jean frequently invited our three sons to come into her room. Sitting on the floor, they gained the wisdom of ninety-plus years. She had a heart for missions and a sincere love for the Lord. Our sons were infused.

She brought an abundance of joy and laughter to the dinner table and filled our home with her charm and grace. From her treasury of godly wisdom, she gave welcomed counsel to my wife and me on several occasions. She was an intimate part of our family for over twenty years, happily passing into the arms of Jesus at 103. No ice floe here. Having Nana Jean in our family, as indeed *she was family*, was what the Lord wanted for us.

Although our family situation was special—perhaps unique—Nana Jean was our priority. To have her live elsewhere was beyond our thought. She was our *queen* and much loved. We were blessed to have Jean be with us to the end of her earthbound life.

Ripples of her life touched many during her remaining years and beyond. Her life continues to inspire me and my three sons, who are now approaching their own Autumn of Life. People matter to God. The more people matter to us, the more we become like Jesus.

> . . . *standing by the cross of Jesus were his mother and his mother's sister, Mary the wife of Clopas, and Mary Magdalene. When Jesus saw his mother and the disciple whom he loved standing nearby, he said to his mother, "Woman, behold, your son!" Then he said to the disciple, "Behold, your mother!" And from that hour the disciple took her to his own home. John 19:25–27*

* * * *

Let's Be Friends

Friendships that survived the ups and downs of passing years, forged and molded by time, intimacy, and shared experiences, soon fade in the lives of older adults.

These precious relationships become fewer. Separated by distance, limitations, and time. Even death. Death of spouses and friends only adds to our loneliness. This aloneness, too, creates a sense of isolation. *The silence of four walls can be deafening for older adults.*

But the Autumn of Life, our senior years, can also be a time to develop new relationships. It is not a time to withdraw into self-imposed isolation. We can learn to nurture new friendships that foster the missing human touch of fading relationships. Building friendships may mean rethinking our attitude and behavior toward others. We may unintentionally exclude them from our lives. We become preoccupied with our own interests. Self-focused.

But it's up to us. People don't always come to us. Take the initiative. Seek out other seniors who want to engage in the fine art of building friendships. Those who enjoy laughter. Maybe a few friendly arguments. Seek those who also want to get to know others. They're there. Look for them! Be patient.

Engaging people means stepping out of our comfort zone and trying activities we would not usually choose. If appropriate, develop friendships with those younger—maybe much younger—than us. Getting to know people is not hard if we take the first step.

"My mom's advice: Make friends with younger people and gravitate to include these young people on your friend's list."[10] Laura Hook

The aim is to develop meaningful friendships. Don't be an outsider. Get to know other seniors. Become part of a group. Be ready to contribute your voice, considering their interest above your own. Attend senior social gatherings. At church, senior centers, and special interest clubs. Become active in volunteer work. Keep looking for that special person to befriend. If you are able, walk with them. Go to coffee with them or share a bite to eat. Enjoy life together. It's therapeutic for you and them. *Start small, grow big!*

Consider the number of times we find Jesus and food. Whenever there was food, He was there to participate in the "breaking of bread." The place where friendships are birthed. Jesus will have great joy when, as a family, we are seated at His table at the Marriage Supper of the Lamb. Food, family, and friends are the divine recipe for healthy relationships. Yes. Particularly for building lasting friendships.

Many of us seem to be busy going somewhere. Yet, as we hurry along, how often do we overlook the growing number of people in our community going nowhere? Alone. Just waiting. Waiting for someone to speak a kind word, call, visit, or take them somewhere—someone who might become a friend. *Friends are so important for them—and for us!*

True Friends

Having friends is needed in our final stage of life. Without friends, living can be very lonely, even for *older couples*. We are not talking about people we know as *contacts* from our phone directory, past business acquaintances, clubs, church, or the many "friends" we collect on Facebook. True friends are what's needed.

True friends are those with whom we have bonded over time and forged a shared path—emotionally, physically, and spiritually. They are people with whom we share genuine life experiences that are sustainable. Unbreakable. They, over time, have been woven into the fabric of our lives. Times of laughter. Times of sorrow. True Friends *(1 Samuel 18:1–4)*.

These friends share a deep respect and steadfast appreciation for one another. Such bonding isn't bothered by gaps in time or geographic distances. Making up for lost time is not needed. The relationship picks up where it left off. Friendships like this must be nourished and protected as we age. True friends sound a lot like *I Corinthians 13:4–7*:

Love is patient and kind; love does not envy or boast; it is not arrogant or rude. It does not insist on its own way; it is not irritable or resentful; it does not rejoice at wrongdoing but rejoices with the truth. Love bears all things, believes all things, hopes all things, endures all things.

We live in a society immersed in shallow acquittances. Investment of time and commitment for long-term relationships don't seem to be a priority. These associations fade in our aging years. We often come up short with true friends. As people enter the Autumn of Life, sustainable, authentic, and durable friendships are what is needed—true friends that are good for a lifetime.

As our aging population increases, so does the number of lonely people. People who are in desperate need of friends—true friends. They are rare. But they are there to be discovered.

The Cost of True Friendships

Enduring friendships cost. Commitment, time, and effort. However, in our culture, few seem willing to invest what is required for durable friendships. Unhappily, our culture teaches us unhealthy patterns of behavior that make relationships momentary and shallow. Simply a means to an end. Rarely pausing long enough to place value on people as *people*. Sadly, what we learn affects our relationships with others. Such relationships rarely go beyond surface encounters. But we need more.

I once had neighbors who were from India. If not for them, my other neighbors would have been strangers. This Indian couple valued people and cultivated friendships by having neighbors gather occasionally to share a meal in their home. They also regularly called to express interest in our welfare. Why? Because friends were important to them—people mattered to them. They embraced that value. They taught me an important lesson about building lasting friendships. Friendships that go-deep cost time, commitment, and a sincere interest in others.

We can talk in general about *all* our "friends" while remaining desperately alone—alone, without a true soul mate. But a true friend—a soul mate—takes time and effort to develop. Giving ourselves to another. It's not easy. It requires learning to be less self-focused and increasingly more interested in others. Yes. It takes work but it's worth the effort.

Not all attempts to make friends are successful. A relationship may continue for some time without becoming a true friend. That's okay. Remember, friendships are based on *mutual* commitment. A mutual willingness to open-up. Become vulnerable. If mutual resolve and commitment exist, the relationship will succeed, and a new friend will be added to our social calendar. In the meantime, keep up the search.

Cultivating friends takes time. Don't be in a hurry. It's like growing a garden. Prepare the ground by selecting opportunities. Enrich the soil to help make things grow by investing time and effort. Plant seeds of kindness with helpful words and deeds. Then, patiently wait for a relationship to sprout, producing blossoms of mutual joy and satisfaction.

The story is told of a farmer who returns home after a hot and tiring day in the field. He entered the house and found his wife distraught, bathed in a pool of tears.

"Mary Lou, is something wrong?"

"Yes, Sam. There is something wrong! Very wrong!" Mary Lou replied." "We've been married for twenty years. I've managed the house, cared for the children and you, done the chores, and even helped you in the barn. Cleaning the stalls and tossing hay."

"Yes, that's right," agreed Sam.

"Sam, in all those years, not once have you told me that you loved me."

"Mary Lou," Sam interrupted, "On the day we were married, I told you I loved you. Mary Lou, you'd be the first to know if something were to change."

Such a story would be humorous if not so sadly true for some. Friendships, including marriages, need words that affirm and express appreciation—words of endearment if needed. Not once, but frequently.

Perhaps that's why God tells us He loves us so many times and in so many ways.

Early in our marriage, daily I told my wife that I loved her. At times, in the middle of an argument. A sincere daily "I love you" made for a beautiful marriage. Even when she was overwhelmed with dementia, we still expressed our love for one another.

Friendships require physical, emotional, and spiritual involvement in someone else's life. They need to be open, honest, candid, and vulnerable. Although true friends are rare, they remain important for us in the Autumn of Life. There is still a place and time to make beautiful friendships during our journey as aging seniors. *Let's go out and grow some friends!*

Our Friend

Our most underdeveloped and under-cultivated friendship may be the one with Jesus. As our friend, He committed Himself completely to us. It, too, was costly.

Greater love has no one than this, that someone lay down his life for his friends. You are my friends if you do what I command you. No longer do I call you servants, for the servant does not know what his master is doing; but I have called you friends, for all that I have heard from my Father I have made known to you. John 15:13–15

Rekindling our friendship with Jesus may be harder as we grow older. Life seems rigid. Demanding. And less open to spiritual realities. As we age, we may become cynical, argumentative, and frustrated with the Church—*and God*. We can become angry with our physical and emotional limitations, the lack of attention and interaction with our families, and a host of other annoyances. However, the words of a favorite hymn, *What a Friend We Have in Jesus*, remind us of His constant, unchanging friendship with us as we share every adversity with Him:

What a Friend we have in Jesus,
All our sins and griefs to bear!
What a privilege to carry
Everything to God in prayer!
O what peace we often forfeit,
O what needless pain we bear,
All because we do not carry
Everything to God in prayer!
Joseph M. Scriven (1855), Public Domain

It takes discipline and intention to nurture our relationship with Jesus. He is our Lord, but He is also our Friend. Not only does our friendship with Him need to be nurtured, but it must also become active.

We may agree that people need God. Yes! But *people also need people*. We are the hands, feet, smile, and words of Jesus for others—our spouse, families, and friends—to everyone God puts in our path to bless *today!*

As we peek under the curtain, we are amazed to see what is going on in heaven. Heaven is all about relationships. First and foremost, we have a relationship with Jesus, our faithful friend. Then, with each other. We will have all of eternity to discover and develop new relationships. New friends. Millions of them!

After this I looked, and behold, a great multitude that no one could number, from every nation, from all tribes and peoples and languages, standing before the throne and before the Lamb, clothed in white robes, with palm branches in their hands, and crying out with a loud voice, "Salvation belongs to our God who sits on the throne, and to the Lamb!"
Revelation 7:9–11

But let's not wait until heaven to begin building relationships. It may be a challenge. But it can be done. Let's come out of our self-imposed seclusion and engage others with the joy Jesus gives. Begin to show and speak words of kindness, mercy, peace, and grace to a world darkened by sin. *That's exciting!*

Unless God intervenes, twisted, broken, and separated relationships may not be recoverable this side of heaven. Only He knows how to mend them. Pray. But God is a God of new beginnings. Relationships can be beautiful, positive, and productive as your contacts with others are infused with His presence. As they flourish and blossom into friendships, they become His gift of aging.

So many people come into our lives then leave the way they came. But there are those precious few who touch our hearts so deeply we will never be the same.
— *Mary Engelbreit*

* * * *

Remember my affliction and my wanderings,
the wormwood and the gall!
My soul continually remembers it
and is bowed down within me.
But this I call to mind,
and therefore, I have hope:

The steadfast love of the LORD never ceases.
His mercies never come to an end.
They are new every morning.
Great is your faithfulness.

"The LORD is my portion," says my soul,
"Therefore, I will hope in him."
The Lord is good to those who wait for him,
to the soul who seeks him.
Lamentations 3:19–25

Let's Talk About It

1. *How would you describe your relationship with your family and friends? Are you pleased with those relationships? What can you do to improve those relationships?*

2. *Do you feel alone, like being on an ice floe, even when family and friends are nearby? Explain.*

3. *How do you distinguish between friends and "true" friends? Explain.*

4. *Describe your true friends—your "soul-mate friends." How have they become true friends?*

5. *Though Jesus is Lord, Creator of all, how do you know Jesus is your friend?*

. . . God is love. In this the love of God was made manifest among us, that God sent his only Son into the world, so that we might live through him. In this is love, not that we have loved God but that he loved us and sent his Son to be the propitiation for our sins. Beloved, if God so loved us, we also ought to love one another. 1 John 4:8–11

Looking Ahead

In the next Chapter, we will see how the Autumn of Life challenges many older adults. This season of life becomes a time for many to face fresh adversities. Like trees that lose leaves in Autumn, we, too, will experience loss—letting go.

Together, we will encounter God, who created the seasons *(Genesis 1:14)*. Each one designed to show Himself in special ways to us. But this season, the Autumn of Life, is of special importance to those of us who are older. Let's find out how God can transform our challenges into His gift of aging.

8

The Autumn of Life

Here we are. In the Autumn of Life. The season before Winter when life seems to sleep. Bees, birds, and bears all find their quiet retreat until the warmth of Spring awakens them from their slumber.

But in Autumn, the lush green of grass and trees send their message of change, of letting go, and preparation. A transforming beauty descends quietly upon the earth in a tapestry of vibrant colors as trees surrender their crowns to the waiting earth below.

It is time to think seriously about the days God still allots to us. A time to prepare for what is coming. The message is clear: Time is short! As we age, navigating through this season can be a challenge. We will look at a few of these challenges the Autumn of Life has prepared for us.

Understanding Seasons

T he oscillating rhythms of earth provide the annual seasons of Spring, Summer, Autumn, and Winter. For many living near the equator, such movement produces only wet and dry seasons. The Bible tells us God determined how we experience these cycles of life *(Genesis 1:14–15)*. But Autumn is a special season. It has much to say to us about life. Our life. Aging.

In a recent article posted on LinkedIn (October 31.2023), *Autumn's Meaning in Life: Three Life Lessons from The Fall Season*, Tina Swain shares her insightful thoughts about Autumn.

> In Autumn, *"nature whispers its timeless wisdom, inviting us to reflect on the deeper meanings and life lessons that this magical time of year bestows upon us . . .*
>
> *"Embracing (Autumn) can be a powerful teacher, urging us to embrace change, letting go of what no longer serves us, and find beauty in the impermanence of life . . .*
>
> *"Autumn's arrival marks a time of change, as nature gracefully embraces the cycle of renewal. Similarly, life presents us with a myriad of transitions - some anticipated, while others catch us by surprise . . .*
>
> *"As Autumn settles in, we witness nature's graceful surrender to change."* [11]

Although the end of Autumn is predictable, the message of Autumn exhibits variegated colors of vegetation hastily surrendering to barren branches with abrupt changes in weather. From pleasant days to those requiring additional clothing. We who are older agree with the message of Autumn. Autumn speaks to us. In this season of life, like the surrendering vegetation around us, we see change. The unforgiving change to our bodies, relationships with family and friends, the workplace that is no more—loss and letting go—our surrender to change becomes our shared experience. Like the season, we may feel only barren branches are left.

Many things arrive daily on our doorstep during the Autumn of Life. New, strange, and challenging. Each in its own time and way. Some welcomed. Others not.

King Solomon saw these seasonal events as predictable. Not by a calendar or personal wish to make it so but as an appointed time assigned by loving God. All, to lead us to Himself:

For everything there is a season,
a time for every activity under heaven.
A time to be born and a time to die.
A time to plant and a time to harvest.
A time to kill and a time to heal.
A time to tear down and a time to build up.
A time to cry and a time to laugh.
A time to grieve and a time to dance.
A time to scatter stones and a time to gather stones.
A time to embrace and a time to turn away.

A time to search and a time to quit searching.
A time to keep and a time to throw away.
A time to tear and a time to mend.
A time to be quiet and a time to speak.
A time to love and a time to hate.
A time for war and a time for peace.
What do people really get for all their hard work?
I have seen the burden God has placed on us all.
Yet God has made everything beautiful for its own time.
He has planted eternity in the human heart,
but even so, people cannot see the whole scope of God's work
from beginning to end. Ecclesiastes 3:1–11

A person once shared with me that life is often like a jigsaw puzzle with assorted pieces scattered before us. Only the obvious straight-edged pieces are in place. We tirelessly struggle and grope to find the right puzzle piece that might fit within the frame of our life, but often it doesn't match. At times, we fumble in the dark, blindfolded to God's plan. And sadly, our puzzle didn't come with a completed picture to follow. Often, at the end of life, we are convinced some pieces are missing. Like a jigsaw puzzle, this season of life can be confusing and challenging.

Let's look at some of those challenges that frequent our doorstep in the Autumn of Life.

A Season to Suffer

Suffering is a season, an appointed time, often repeated throughout life. Sometimes briefly. Other times, the season lingers. Older people, however, may encounter suffering more frequently, intensely, and for extended periods. Physical afflictions, mental disorders, and emotional grief and pain often strike in the Autumn of Life. Such uncertainties make this season of life a challenge.

Suffering is never pleasant but never without purpose—a divine purpose. Suffering has an appointed time, a season, to produce the desired result of making us more like Christ. It is His opportunity to eliminate debris and clutter from our lives so He can occupy our lives more fully. In the same way, our appointed time with our dentist is rarely a pleasant experience. However, the beneficial outcome outweighs the pain and discomfort. God, like the dentist, knows what He is doing.

God desires to achieve a beneficial outcome for our lives through suffering. He seeks what is best for us, though not always wrapped in roses and sweetness *(2 Corinthians 12:7–10)*. (See Chapter 3, page 47)

A Season for Ending a Career

Ending a career begins an uncertain journey for many. It's called retirement. This journey is like entering a fog bank with limited vision. The anticipated path can be strewn with unseen and bewildering obstacles.

This journey started the day we said goodbye to our friends. The people we worked with. We enjoyed the farewell lunch, the gifts, cards, and well-wishes. We thanked the boss for the achievement awards. With the exit interview completed, we turned in our keys, signed the separation papers, and cleared our desk.

With cardboard box in hand, and the security guard holding the door, we left the building. We then scanned the parking lot. Emotional shock of finality clouded our memory. "Now, where did I park the car?"

Leaving the parking lot and heading home, a sense of loss punctuated by an uneasy freedom engulfs us. Uncertainty. Thus, a new season of life is birthed.

It can be traumatic. Not only have we lost the sense of security and predictability our job provided, but the familiar routine of going to work, morning office coffee, and yakking with co-workers is also gone. We may feel we lost our identity, self-worth, and purpose. We might feel alone, like a ship at sea, without anchor or rudder.

Much of what we did in the workplace identified who we were. *I was an engineer, teacher, nurse, manager, etc.* But no more! Now, I'm just me.

The emotional stress of no longer needing to be employed can be a significant loss. When we see how easily our job title, tasks, and perceived importance of our position were quickly given to someone else, we may wonder how important we were to the company. What we were fades to a distant memory in the minds of those left behind. We face the challenge of reduced income and wondering how we will make it.

Sometimes, searching in vain for a niche to chart a new path or doing nothing can feel like a divorce or losing a loved one. Recovery from this loss may take months or even years.

But such a season of life may be God's appointed time for discovery—finding a new you. Consider Moses *(Exodus 3; 4:17)*. Coming to the end of his career as a shepherd, God handed him something new to do.

As an older man of eighty years, Moses prepared to settle into a quiet job of shepherding sheep. But God had a different plan. One day, while caring for his sheep, God met him in a burning bush—God's appointed time for Moses. There, he discovered that God had something else for him to do. Among the many things God told Moses, one is significant. God asked Moses, "What is in your hand?" "A staff," Moses replied.

A staff. This staff symbolized Moses' identity and self-worth as a forty-year career shepherd. But God told him to let it go. Throw it on the ground. I will transform what is in your hand into something far more glorious, powerful, and infused with My authority. It became the Staff of God. A staff to do miracles, to cause Pharoah to let God's people go, to open a path through the sea, and to shepherd a different kind of sheep—millions of God's people through a wilderness. Letting go meant letting God be all Moses needed for this new season of life.

Coming to the end of our career is not the time to settle down to a quiet life under the stars, but rather a time to meet with God in a unique way. A time to hear God ask, "What is in your hand?" God wants to transform our staff powerfully to affect the lives of others for His kingdom.

Some older people are retired but, in their minds, have never left their jobs. They continue to live as in the former days when they were employed. They speak frequently of what they were and what they did. Living in the past but never quite in the present. Perhaps they are fearful of losing their identity and self-worth or being the person today they truly are—without their "staff."

Retirement can be God's appointed time to discover the gifts He has given us to do a greater work to advance His kingdom. Discover what they are. Go forward with His staff in hand and use what He has given us for His work. Remember, He seeks to transform what was in our hand into something far greater than we can imagine. It's His special gift to us— the gift of aging.

A Season for Letting Go

"In Autumn's spectacle of falling leaves, we find a powerful metaphor for letting go . . . trees release their leaves, surrendering to the flow of nature.

"Letting go is not a sign of weakness but an act of courage and wisdom. In life, we often cling to things, beliefs, or relationships that no longer nourish our souls. Autumn teaches us the importance of shedding what no longer serves us, creating space for new growth and possibilities.

"Just as nature sheds its leaves, we can declutter our lives, releasing physical and emotional burdens that weigh us down . . . Letting go becomes an act of liberation, allowing us to create space for personal growth, fresh insights, and boundless possibilities." (Tina Swain)[12]

Letting go is a significant part of aging and undoubtedly one of the hardest things to do. We possess an instinctive desire to cling to things and people. It's hard to let go!

The following story illustrates how difficult it is to "let go:"

A man, walking too close to the edge of a cliff, fell, plummeting toward pounding surf and jagged rocks below. Thankfully, he broke his fall by grabbing hold of a bush on his way to certain death. He yelled for help! Eventually, he heard someone on top of the cliff. "Who is up there?" he cried out in desperation. "Jesus," came the reply. Following a short moment of reflection, the man called out again, "Jesus, can you help me?"

"Yes, I can."

"Well, Jesus, what do you want me to do?"

"Let go!" Jesus replied.

Letting go can challenge our whole being. As illustrated above, letting go can be a dramatic leap of faith. Can God be trusted? This insightful question speaks deeply to our soul.

Letting go signals the Autumn of Life when things and people, like leaves on a tree, begin to fall away. Soon, they are no more. Letting go may create an irreplaceable loss. But letting go is often the beginning of a new you.

Letting Go of Things

Disasters like floods, fire, earthquakes, tornados, wars, and thieves rob us of our things. The loss of all that touched our lives—even loved ones. What remains is a pile of scattered rubble and ashes.

For many, particularly older people, such extreme loss is devastating. The end of what we valued. Everything that defined who we were is now gone. We may conclude our life is over. There's nothing more to live for.

Others see the pile of ruin and ashes simply as stuff. For them, it is a time to begin again. The beginning of a new season of life. Yes. It is sad to lose family photos and irreplaceable mementos of the past. Looking at what is no more, they decide it is time to move on to rebuild their lives anew.

For older people, the loss of cherished things comes at an emotional cost. Moving to smaller quarters is a challenge. Unwilling to face the reality for a smaller footprint can result in small apartments overwhelmed with clutter gathered over the years. Purging things means precious memories become like Autumn leaves. They must go. There is no more room.

During a recent move to a smaller apartment, I learned the challenge of "holy surrender." Of letting go. I had to release many things I held dear, particularly those with deep family roots.

Three plastic plates that captured my sons' first attempts at being artists on which they painted their love for Mommie and Daddy were included. Boxes of family photos. Who really bothers looking at old family photos anymore? And there was more.

As mental and emotional fog settled in, I hauled the same objects from room to room, unsure about what to do with them. Yet haunted by this fact: I was moving from two bedrooms to one, my world was getting smaller and simpler.

In "holy surrender," I learned to give back to God the things He has given me. But I found this harder to do at my age. Facing the reality of "smaller," I concluded: this, too, will pass and soon I will see all God has in store for me—and others.

Thankfully, my children rescued me from my dilemma. They happily became recipients of my surrender—of letting go. Even though they will face the same dilemma when they enter the Autumn of their lives. The plastic plates? I returned them as Christmas presents to the original artists. They were delighted!

Many things that helped us remember the pleasures of a past life quickly become Autumn leaves. Family and younger friends remind us there is no room to keep everything. Alone in our small apartment with a few acquaintances down the hall. Is this what Autumn is about? *Bare branches!*

The loss is great when older adults stubbornly cling to the past and obsess over memories, experiences, and stuff. Depression, bitterness, and angst toward God may result. Holy surrender is far from their minds.

Others in their senior years will view their loss of things differently. Yes. Sad, as when Autumn leaves have fallen, yet thankful. Although walls have grown closer and places to put things fewer, they carry on renewed in the knowledge that God has appointed a time, a season, for shedding. A time of letting go. They understand that letting go and loss are preparing them to leave this earth to be with Jesus in heaven, where there is nothing to cling to except Him.

As in the past when Grandpa and Grandma could no longer ride horses, giving up the "car keys" means another leaf has fallen to the ground. Personal freedoms may be curtailed if deemed unsafe by the family. Our freedoms shrink! How well we accept these new boundaries is critical to our ability to accept the Autumn of Life with thankfulness.

Learning to accept God's appointed time, designed by Him for our benefit, can be challenging. Not all appointed times are pleasant. This, too, is a challenge. Yet, whatever we lose in this life, God replaces it with Himself, transforming our experience into a gift of aging.

Letting Go of Friends and Loved Ones

Our longevity sometimes outlives friends and loved ones, creating a sense of deep loss and loneliness.

In her 90s, Nana Jean traveled several thousand miles yearly to visit friends and family. This annual migration stopped when, within the space of a few years, her friends and family died. She had no one to see. Traveling alone by air became more challenging. So, Jean, being the person she was, pursued other ventures.

But many people are not as robust as Jean. They may fall into depression and feel alone in a world that neither cares nor makes time for them. It is a season of loss. It hurts and hurts deeply!

The death of a spouse can be devastating. Grieving never entirely leaves us. It lingers. Erupting at strange times and in unexpected places. Grieving can bring not only tears of sorrow but tears of joy. That's okay.

Over time, however, as we heal, grieving brings our heart into the presence of Jesus. Although He wept with others at Lazarus' grave, He declares Himself to be the Resurrection and the Life. He understands our pain and how to comfort the hurting and lonely with joy and peace that is uniquely His.

God's grace enters our grief and wraps us in His love. Our shed tears are mixed with His as He mends our broken heart. We grieve, but not like those with no eternal hope *(1 Thessalonians 4:13–18)*. Because God's grace can transform our grief and loss into an offering to Him—the gift of aging.

A Season for Becoming Yourself
by Paula Freeman

Get away with me and you'll recover your life . . .
Walk with me and work with me—watch how I
do it. Learn the unforced rhythms of grace.
Matthew 11:28-29, MSG

By the time we reach the Autumn of Life, we've persevered through decades of adulthood. Responsibilities to fulfill. Roles to play. Images to maintain. Many of us, however, have lost touch with ourselves along the way—our longings, dreams, and passions—maybe even our compass. But in the Autumn of Life, we have fewer distractions and more personal time. Time to reflect on our life. To tend things that have been left undone. To peel off the masks. To consider the things of God and His sufficiency as we age. Time to become the person Jesus created us to be.

A season for becoming yourself is about saying "yes" to Jesus' invitation to "Follow me . . . I want to recover your life." It's active. Intentional. Counter-cultural. It's a process. Here we wrestle down apathy. Transform habits. And defeat resignation to old habits and familiar ways. A season for becoming yourself is rooted in the knowledge that God has numbered our days (and there are now fewer of them!) But it was born in our Father's heart. Although our paths may be littered with brokenness, grief, regret, and striving, it is never too late. Our true self, the life that Jesus recovers, is a gift of grace that transforms us, so we become more like Jesus within the unique boundaries of our personhood.

In his book, *God Walk: Moving at the Speed of Your Soul*, author Mark Buchanan says: "The mimicry that Jesus invites us to—follow Me, learn from Me, take My yoke upon you—never distorts our personality; it releases it. We become more ourselves by becoming more like Jesus . . . We lose our life but gain it. We speak His words and find our voice. We walk in His ways and hit our stride. We conform to His character and discover our true selves. We submit to His will and stop being slaves to everyone else's, our own especially . . . Maybe no one truly becomes themselves—wholly, freely, unreservedly, not needing to be someone else— until we walk long enough with Jesus that we become as He is."[13]

Where earlier seasons were marked by striving and productivity, the season for becoming yourself is about believing and receiving. No formula or how-to manual.

Only a person: His name is Jesus. And while His recovery process for every person is unique, there are consistent themes that declare themselves.

We claim our identity in Jesus Christ. His Holy Spirit transforms our hearts and minds to become more like Jesus for the sake of others. Prayer changes us: words become few, and we desire to align our will with God's will. Surrender defines the posture of our heart, repentance, deep, and sincere. Solitude nourishes our spiritual life. Integration of head and heart allows us to experience God's presence in deep, satisfying ways. We learn then practice spiritual disciplines to help us know God more. Gratitude grows. The need to control diminishes and contentment increases. Compassion takes root. Pretense, image, and pride begin to wane. Grace for self and others flows from a heart made new. Generosity increases. Self-sufficiency is replaced by God-dependency *(Ephesians 4:17–24)*.

Because Jesus lives in each believer *(Galatians 2:20)*, His invitation to follow Him invites us to know Him more. And, in so doing, we begin to discover who we really are in Christ. In Him, we learn surrender the facade of who we are not and rescue our true identity in Him. We find the gift of aging.

A Season for Prayer and Devotion

Our senior years are a season for doing less. No more careers to consume our time. Less distractions. The constant challenge of raising a family is gone. But as aging seniors, we often fill our time with everything except God. Activities, meetings, and seemingly endless conversations with others. All good! But not when our schedules allow no room for what is eternally important. *We are all moving closer to eternity.*

We have more time to talk with God in our senior years. Focused, yet informal prayer. Scripture tells us to pray without ceasing. It is good to speak with God throughout the day. But let's not neglect the *season* of prayer where intimacy with God is the focus. Such prayer takes time, practice, and discipline.

As we pray, let our spirit rest quietly in His presence. Discover God in the holy place—the sanctuary where He is enthroned. Our only right of entrance into the presence of God is by grace through the blood of Jesus Christ. In that place, God invites us to touch the untouchable and handle the holy things of His eternal presence:

One thing have I asked of the Lord, that will I seek after: that I may dwell in the house of the Lord all the days of my life, to gaze upon the beauty of the Lord and to inquire[2] in his temple.

. . . and I will offer in his tent sacrifices with shouts of joy. I will sing and make melody to the Lord.

You have said, "Seek my face." My heart says to you, "Your face, LORD, do I seek." Psalm 27:4, 6, 8

Some may argue that such praying is "too much God." But for most of us, at best, we are only a few short years from being in God's presence. Beyond these few short years, "too much God" does not exist. Soon, we will be in His presence, where He will be all in all. *That's a lot of God!*

Learn to pray while reading the Bible. Talk to Him about what He is saying. Such reading of Scripture can be transforming.

Pray for others. Let prayer become a gateway into the lives of others. Find out what can be done about their situation. Their need. Rejoice with them that rejoice and weep with them who weep, whether they are thanking the Lord or hurting *(Romans 12:15).*

Lastly, stay engaged with those for whom we pray. Follow up. Ask how things are going. Then, reshape your prayers to target their need better.

Prayer is an appointed time. Learn to keep the ears of our souls open to what the Lord is saying to us during our season of devotion. Stay with it.

Setting aside time to pray in the presence of God will free us from a *ho-hum* prayer life and transform it into the gift of aging—one that prepares us to enjoy an eternity with Him.

A Season for Joy and Thankfulness

Prayer and devotion to Christ brings us into a season of joy and thankfulness. These two attributes are gifts from the throne of God. Not engineered, manufactured, or produced by human effort. Joy and thankfulness for *all things,* including afflictions and adversities, come from God. Only those who know God can express this apparent contradiction in a single breath.

Always be joyful. Never stop praying. Be thankful in all circumstances, for this is God's will for you who belong to Christ Jesus. 1 Thessalonians 5:16–18, NLT, emphasis added

Too often, faces of older Christians express gloom and doom as though the world had ended, and they were left behind. Joy and thankfulness have disappeared from their lives. What remains is a sense of drudgery. Christian duty to be endured until they make it to their grave. *"A joyful heart is good medicine, but a crushed spirit dries up the bones"* (Proverbs 17:22).

Not experiencing joy and thankfulness as part of our faith-walk is a measure of missing intimacy with Jesus. To live in the awareness of His presence, to converse with Him along the way, means we will get what He has—His joy:

These things I have spoken to you, that my joy may be in you, and that your joy may be full. John 15:11

Joy and thankfulness are possible when we face afflictions, adversity, and troubles. It flows like a river from Him to us. It's a mystery, yet totally available!

"Joy emerges from the ashes of adversity through your trust and thankfulness." Sarah Young[14]

Heaven is bathed in joy and thankfulness. The question of sin is off the table as a child of God. Our sin is forgiven, forgotten, forever, Amen! *(Jeremiah 31:34)*. When we meditate on the wonder of this truth, our only response is to *rejoice and be thankful!*

Jesus, our shepherd, cares for us constantly and loves us completely. We are his precious possession. We are in Him. Kept and secure! *"I will never leave you nor forsake you" Psalm 23; Hebrews 13:5–6*. Rejoice and be thankful!

Consider the Lord's joy over us—He can hardly contain Himself:

The Lord your God is in your midst, a mighty one who will save; he will rejoice over you with gladness; he will quiet you by his love; he will exult over you with loud singing.
Zephaniah 3:17, emphasis added

Rejoice and be thankful!

The moment we awaken in the morning ushers us into a new day. But best of all, we are one day closer to seeing Jesus face to face, where we will praise Him without our disabilities or limitations, filled with joy and thanksgiving throughout eternity. We are His child. Think of it! A child of the King of kings and Lord of lords. Royalty! *(1 Peter 2:9–10).* Rejoice and be thankful!

For you shall go out in joy and be led forth in peace;
the mountains and the hills before you shall break forth into
singing, and all the trees of the field shall clap their hands.
Isaiah 55:12

Thank Him throughout the day for the big and small things, the "good" and the "bad." Learn to laugh more. Don't take yourself too seriously. The Lord knows we are human with all our imperfections and weaknesses. Physically, we are dust, and to dust we will return. Our earthly body is only temporary *(2 Corinthians 4:16–18).* Praise the Lord! Be patient! We'll soon get a new one!

Be joyful, knowing whose we are and where we are going. Spend time with joyful people—they're contagious. Let's look at ourselves in the mirror and smile at what we see. Rejoice and be thankful!

A sovereign, loving God has stamped His image upon our lives. Don't worry about today or tomorrow. He controls everything: our loved ones, the world, and *us*. Rejoice and be thankful! (*Matthew 6:25–34; Philippians 4:5–7)*

* * * *

Concluding Thoughts

The Autumn of Life is a season for change, letting go, and preparing. At times, deeply challenging yet liberating. How we navigate this season affects life now and beyond. We are only aging adults for a short time. Navigate well the present but prepare for the future.

Time deceives us. It is not our friend. It can lull our minds to eternal realities. This season will soon end. Not only will the leaves fade and fall but they will disappear. We will pass from this life into the next. God has promised eternal life with Him to those who believe in Jesus Christ *(John 3:16)*. The missing puzzle piece is found. *The greatest gift of aging.*

Let's Talk About It

1. *How does your time and God's time differ? Discuss how this has affected your life. Talk about the seasons of life you have experienced.*

2. *What experience have you had in "letting go" of things or people as an older person? How have you dealt with that?*

3. *What things interfer with your desire to pray and pursue an intimate time with the Lord? What can you do to correct these interferences?*

4. *What keeps you from being joyful and thankful for all things as the Scripture teach? How has God helped you learn joy and thankfulness?*

Rejoice in the Lord always; <u>again</u>,
I will say, rejoice.
Philippians 4:4, emphasis added

Looking Ahead

In our final Chapter, we reflect on the gift of aging. We get one shot at aging. We want to do it right. We will review the important issues of how to navigate growing old—what we covered in the previous eight chapters.

God makes no mistakes. He is in control regardless of our state, physically, mentally, or emotionally. Nothing happens without passing the test of His love. In that light, we will put the finishing touches on how God transforms the challenges of growing old as His gift of aging.

As I Face the Wilderness

Lord, as I face the wilderness
Give me strength to bear the load,
And patience to endure the places
Where there is no road.

Give me eyes, your pillar of fire, to see
Amidst my darkest night;
To know each painful thorn and cutting stone
Prepared by You who always do what is right

For others who journey this common path
Give me shoulders their burden to bear,
Who often stumble like myself,
A comforting word and a tear to share.

But most, give me a heart
That hungers and thirsts for you,
Lord, as I face the wilderness
To be fashioned and molded anew.

—Don Zoller January 1998

The Gift of Aging

Join me before the mirror of truth. What we see are two old people growing older. This is simply aging. No matter what we tell ourselves or what we may do to halt the aging process, it cannot be stopped. Our bodies are tired, and many vital functions don't work like they used to. Our youthful vigor and strength are running on the low end of half-full.

Aging gracefully requires more than putting on a happy face. That doesn't work. It's about changing our heart attitude before God. And being at peace with whatever may come our way because we know it first passes through His hands of love for us. This new attitude is His gift of aging!

It's All About Aging—God's Way

G rowing old need not be a negative experience. Something we wish would go away. How could a reasonable person think that pain, suffering, grief, and other challenges of aging could be considered a gift? Adversities abound. *Get real!*

We've looked at some aging challenges and recognized them as our own. Huge and unforgiving. But we've also seen how God provides a way for older adults to navigate these challenges and grow to see them as a gift. Whenever adversity arrives on our doorstep, it becomes a burdensome drudgery without the presence of God.

But aging does not need to be a drudgery. While flooded with adversities accompanying aging, we can discover how to anchor our hope to the One who loves us perfectly and knows what He is doing.

Pause, reflect, and chart a new path. Each step uneven and uncertain. Yet confident, they are designed by God, who makes no mistakes in judgment nor action, bathing each pain in His love.

Even though I walk through the valley of the shadow of death, I will fear no evil, for you are with me; your rod and staff, they comfort me. Psalm 23:4

Our faith, our trust in God's passionate love for us, will help us deal with the multitude of adversities that assault us in aging, whether acute or chronic. They challenge our bodies, emotions, and many times, our faith. Pain that so often comes with suffering is real and disturbing. Physical limitations and grief impair our desire to do more. Frustration abounds.

But God invites us to climb out of our pit of difficulty and self-pity. To encounter Him at *the burning bush*, as Moses did, to experience what He has planned for our lives to further His glory. And, like Myrna and Jean, to be a blessing to others.

Climbing out of our pit is hard! Very hard! But God's secure hand is always there when we *let go* and allow Him to embrace us in His love. And extend to us His blessing, *"Well done good and faithful servant."*

Faith, Mighty Faith

Faith, mighty faith, the promise sees,
And looks to God alone;
Laughs at impossibilities,
And cries it shall be done!
And cries it shall be done!

Charles Wesley, 1707–1788
Public Domain

"Listen to me, O house of Jacob,
all the remnant of the house of Israel,
who have been borne by me from before your birth,
carried from the womb:
Even to your old age I am he,
and to gray hairs I will carry you.
I have made, and I will bear.
I will carry and will save." Isaiah 46:3–4

Practical Help for Aging

At our age, we need all the help we can get. Here are some practical helps for aging and aging well:

- Keep your Bible handy. Read it daily. Learn the joy of discovery. *We still don't know it all!*

- Keep praying—for intimacy with God, His kingdom work, for others, and yourself. He whispers to you as you pray and read His Word. Listen to Him. A gentle wind. *His voice is small and quiet* but *transforming!*

- Listen to music to brighten your spirits. Particularly music that inspires you to worship Jesus, be it hymns or gospel songs. Or quiet sounds for meditation. Don't stop singing. Even though your voice may sound terrible to others, it is always pleasant to Jesus.

- Laugh more at your problems, frailties, and yourself. Invite God to join you in your laughter.

His joy, along with ours, will one day fill the corridors of heaven. *Rejoice in the Lord, and again I will say rejoice (Philippians 4:4–7).*

- Be thankful. In and for all things. For others and for God. A thankful spirit drives away the darkness of introspection, self-pity, and complaining. *Thankfulness wins with God.*

- Trust God. He is not only "The God of the Mountain" but also "The God of the Valley." He will guide and guard you. He will show you how to navigate your aging years. *I will never leave you nor forsake you Hebrews 13:5–6.*

- Be creative. God is. Learn from Him what you can do to bless others despite your limitations.

Not that I am speaking of being in need, for I have learned in whatever situation I am to be content. I know how to be brought low, and I know how to abound. In any and every circumstance, I have learned the secret of facing plenty and hunger, abundance and need. I can do all things through him who strengthens me.
Philippians 4:11–13

- Engage the people you meet. Those who wish to talk. Those who are alone. Those who are in need.

- Talk to yourself—out loud. It helps. As you navigate about the house from room to room you will find you are your best guide for what comes next. Talking to yourself is allowed at our age.

Because of the tender mercy of our God, whereby the sunrise shall visit us from on high to give light to those who sit in darkness and in the shadow of death, to guide our feet into the way of peace. (Luke 1:78–79

Today is the oldest you've ever been, yet the youngest you'll ever be. So, enjoy this day while it lasts.[15]
Morning Star

Aging is A Gift

Yes, aging is a gift. A God-given gift especially for you. How you receive His gift, how you use it determines the kind of image you see in your mirror. An image of a defeated old person or an old person who smiles at possibilities. To think, God has blessed you with the gray hair of wisdom, wrinkles of experience, and the spirit of joy to share with others until your time on earth ends, to begin anew with Christ above.

Look into your mirror again. Yes. You're old. But there is Someone next to you also looking at your reflection. He speaks. "You are beautiful, you are beautiful to me. I am delighted with what I see. For in your mirror, I see a reflection of my Son. Christ in you. One day, you will see what I see. One day, beyond your thought or imagination, you will see Him face to face and be like Him. Filled with great and *forever* joy. I promise." *Song of Solomon 4:1, Isaiah 53:11, 1 John 3:2–3*

But one thing I do: forgetting what lies behind and straining forward to what lies ahead, <u>I press on toward the goal</u> for the prize of the upward call of God in Christ Jesus.
Philippians 3:13–14, emphasis added

But our citizenship is in heaven, and from it we await a Savior, the Lord Jesus Christ, <u>who will transform our lowly body</u> to be like his glorious body, by the power that enables him even to subject all things to himself. Philippians 3:20–21, emphasis added

The Gift of Aging is not the end of your story but the beginning of a new chapter in the eternal story of you and your Lord. Forever full of joy, praise, and blessing. Amen!

For those of us in the Autumn of Life who want to know what's next beyond the Gift of Aging, beyond the wrinkles and sagging skin, I highly recommend the book, *Heaven* by Randy Alcorn, Tyndale Momentum, 2004, Carol Stream, Illinois. Available at online book retailers.

What no eye has seen
Nor ear heard
Nor the heart of man imagined.
What God has prepared
For those who love Him.
1 Corinthians 2:9

Let's Talk About It

1. Now that you've read The Gift of Aging, what are your impressions, thoughts, and challenges?

2. What other things would you do as Practical Helps? Are there any helps on the list you see as unneeded?

3. How has reading this book changed your view and understanding of what it means to grow old God's way?

4. Based on what you read, what changes do you plan to make? How and when will you begin?

And we all, with unveiled face,
beholding the glory of the Lord,
are being transformed into the same image
from one degree of glory to another.
For this comes from the Lord who is the Spirit.
2 Corinthians 3:18

Conclusion

Time is short. We don't have much time left. You may be saying, "My body. My mind. My spirit are broken. I can't do it. I can't embrace the Gift of Aging! Oh, yes, you can! You see, the One who was broken for you specializes in broken vessels. Vessels that are cracked and chipped. Utterly broken! Broken people are the ones He is able to work with best. They allow His light within them to shine in the darkness of this world.

In the same way, let your light shine before others, so that they may see your good works and give glory to your Father who is in heaven. Matthew 5:16

Your vessel—your life—no matter how broken, is needed *today*. God is waiting! Your decision, your faith, to trust God for the rest of your life may be only *the size of a mustard seed*, but He is able to transform it into a magnificent tree *(Matthew 13:31–32)*. A tree that provides shade and comfort to those around you. His Gift of Aging is not only for you but for the blessing of others. For the praise of His glory. Amen!

*A **footnote**: Now that you have read the challenges of growing old, reflect. Think how you fit into the story of aging. What changes do you need to make in your life? Pray. Decide. Begin.*

They Still Bear Fruit

The righteous flourish like the palm tree and grow

like a cedar in Lebanon.

They are planted in the house of the Lord;

they flourish in the courts of our God.

They still bear fruit in old age;

they are ever full of sap and green,

to declare that the Lord is upright;

He is my rock, and there is no unrighteousness in him.

Psalm 92:12–15

May the God of hope fill you with all joy and peace in believing, so that by the power of the Holy Spirit you may abound in hope. Roman 15:13

Enough! Up! Out of your rocking chair
(or recliner).
Be the person God has called you to be.

Appendix

What Pleases the Lord Most

Sing to the LORD with thanksgiving;

make melody to our God on the lyre!

He covers the heavens with clouds;

he prepares rain for the earth;

he makes grass grow on the hills.

He gives to the beasts their food,

and to the young ravens that cry.

His delight is not in the strength of the horse,

nor his pleasure in the legs of a man,

but the LORD takes pleasure in those who fear him,

in those who hope in his steadfast love.

Psalm 147:7–11

Appendix 1

A Story of Eternal Perspective

by Aggie Hurst

Back in 1921, a missionary couple named David and Svea Flood left Sweden and traveled to the heart of Africa to the former Belgian Congo with their two-year-old son. There they joined another young Scandinavian couple, the Ericksons. The four of them sought God for specific direction.

Those days were marked with much tenderness, devotion, and sacrifice. Finally, they felt led of the Lord to leave the main mission station to take the gospel to a remote village, the village of N'dolera. This was a huge step of faith.

However, when they arrived at N'dolera, they were rebuffed by the village chief. He would not let them enter his village for fear of alienating the local gods. The two couples opted to go half a mile up the slope and build their own mud huts.

They prayed for a spiritual breakthrough, but there was none. The only contact with the villagers was a young boy, who was allowed to sell them chickens and eggs twice a week. Svea Flood, a tiny woman of only four feet, eight inches tall, decided that if this was the only African she could talk to, she would try to lead the boy to Jesus. And in fact, she succeeded.

But there were no other encouragements. Meanwhile, malaria continued to strike the little band of missionaries one after another. In time, the Ericksons decided they had had enough suffering and decided to return to the main mission station. David and Svea Flood remained near N'dolera to go it alone.

Then Svea found herself pregnant. Of all things. In the middle of this remote and primitive wilderness. When time came for her to give birth, the village chief softened enough to allow a midwife to help her.

A little girl was born, whom they named Aina. The delivery, however, was exhausting. With Svea Flood already weak from bouts of malaria, the birth process only added a heavy and final blow to her stamina. She lasted another seventeen days.

In that moment, something snapped inside David Flood. He dug a crude grave, buried his twenty-seven-year-old wife. He then took his children back down the mountain to the mission station.

Giving his newborn daughter to the Ericksons, he snarled, "I'm going back to Sweden. I've lost my wife, and I obviously can't take care of this baby. God has ruined my life." With that, he headed for the port, rejecting not only his calling, but God Himself.

Within eight months both the Ericksons were stricken with a mysterious sickness and died within days of each other. Baby Aina was then turned over to some American missionaries, who changed her Swedish name to "Aggie." Eventually, they brought her back to the United States. Aggie was three years old.

This family loved the little girl, but they were afraid that if they tried to return to Africa, some legal obstacle might separate her from them. So, they decided to stay in the States and switch from missionary work to pastoral ministry.

And that is how Aggie grew up in South Dakota. As a young woman, she attended North Central Bible college in Minneapolis. There she met and married a young man named Dewey Hurst. Years passed. The Hursts enjoyed a fruitful ministry. Aggie gave birth first to a daughter, then a son.

In time, her husband became president of a Christian college in the Seattle area. Aggie was intrigued to find so much Scandinavian heritage there.

One day a Swedish religious magazine appeared in her mailbox. She had no idea who had sent it, and of course, she couldn't read the words. But as she turned the pages, suddenly, a photo stopped her cold. There in a primitive setting was a grave with a white cross. On the cross were the words SVEA FLOOD.

Aggie jumped in her car and went straight to a college faculty member who could translate the article. "What does this say?" she demanded.

The instructor summarized the story: It was about missionaries who long ago came to a village called N'dolera. The birth of a white baby. The death of the young mother. The one little African boy who had been led to Christ. And how, after the whites had all left, the boy had grown up and finally persuaded the chief to let him build a school in the village. The article said that gradually he won all his students to Christ. And the children led their parents to Christ. Even the chief had become a Christian.

Today there were six hundred Christian believers in that one village. All because of the sacrifice of David and Svea Flood.

For the Hursts' twenty-fifth wedding anniversary, the college presented them with the gift of a vacation to Sweden. There Aggie sought to find her real father.

An old man now, David Flood had remarried, fathered four more children. However, he dissipated his life with alcohol. He also recently had suffered a stroke. Still bitter, he had one rule in his family: "Never mention the name of God—because God took everything from me."

After an emotional reunion with her half-brothers and half-sister, Aggie brought up the subject of seeing her father. The others hesitated. "You can talk to him," they replied, "even though he's very ill now. But you need to know that whenever he hears the name of God, he flies into a rage." Aggie was not to be deterred.

She walked into the squalid apartment, with liquor bottles everywhere, and approached the seventy-three-year-old man lying in a rumpled bed. "Papa?" she said tentatively. He turned and began to cry. "Aina," he said, "I never meant to give you away." "It's all right Papa," she replied, taking him gently in her arms. "God took care of me." The man instantly stiffened. The tears stopped. "God forgot all of us. Our lives have been like this because of Him." He turned his face to the wall.

Aggie stroked his face and then continued, undaunted. "Papa, I've got a little story to tell you, and it's a true one. You didn't go to Africa in vain. Mama didn't die in vain. The little boy you won to the Lord grew up to win that whole village to Jesus Christ. The one seed you planted just kept growing and growing. Today there are six hundred African people serving the Lord because you were faithful to the call of God in your life... "Papa, Jesus loves you. He has never hated you."

The old man turned back to look into his daughter's eyes. His body relaxed. He began to talk. And by the end of the afternoon, he had come back to the God he had resented for so many decades.

Over the next few days, father and daughter enjoyed warm moments together. Aggie and her husband soon had to return to America. Within a few weeks, David Flood had gone into eternity.

A few years later, the Hursts were attending a high-level evangelism conference in London, England, where a report was given from the nation of Zaire (the former Belgian Congo).

The superintendent of the national church, representing some 110,000 baptized believers, spoke eloquently of the gospel's spread in his nation. After his report, Aggie could not help herself in asking him if he had ever heard of David and Svea Flood. "Yes, madam," the man replied in French, his words then being translated into English. "It was Svea Flood who led me to Jesus Christ. I was the boy who brought food to your parents before you were born. In fact, to this day your mother's grave and her memory are honored by all of us." He embraced her in a long, sobbing hug.

Then he continued, "You must come to Africa to see, because your mother is the most famous person in our history." In time, that is exactly what Aggie Hurst and her husband did. They were welcomed by cheering throngs of villagers. She even met the man who had been hired by her father many years before to carry her back down the mountain in a hammock-cradle.

The most dramatic moment, of course, was when the pastor escorted Aggie to see her mother's white cross for herself. She knelt in the soil to pray and give thanks. Later that day, in church, the pastor read from *John 12:24*: *"Verily, verily, I say unto you, except a corn of wheat falls into the ground and dies, it abides alone: but if it dies, it brings forth much fruit."* He then followed with *Psalm 126:5*: *"They that sow in tears shall reap in joy."*

(An edited excerpt from Aggie Hurst, Aggie: The Inspiring Story of A Girl Without A Country [Springfield, MO: Gospel Publishing House, 1986], used by permission.)

It is sometimes difficult to fathom the mysterious, yet magnificent ways of God who in the pit of our suffering, hardships, grief, and sorrow plants the seed of wheat to produce a harvest for His Glory. (Author)

*F*or you shall go out in joy

and be led forth in peace;

the mountains and the hills before you

shall break forth into singing,

and all the trees of the field shall clap their hands.

Instead of the thorn shall come up the cypress;

instead of the brier shall come up the myrtle; and it

shall make a name for the Lord,

an everlasting sign that shall not be cut off."

Isaiah 55:12–13

Appendix 2

The Longest Road

A Poem by Carolyn L. Marcusse
Copyright © 2000

The Longest Road

Sometimes the longest road
   is the one called Wounded.
I walk this way time and again.
Tho' it seems so solitary,
   I see my Savior there before me.
Smiling warmly
   with kindness in His eyes, He says —

   Come and walk here close beside Me.
   I will teach you all my ways.
   The hardest thing is to forgive those
      who will never say they're sorry
      then choose to give the love they don't deserve.
   What you cannot do alone
      the Spirit will accomplish every time
      you walk your longest road.

Sometimes the longest road
   is the one called Forsaken.
Those who promised love have walked away.
It's so hard to be rejected but
   I see my Savior there before me.
Smiling warmly
   with kindness in His eyes, He says —

   Come and walk here close beside Me.
   I will always be your friend.
   I will never leave or forsake you.
   You know, I was rejected too.
   In my Father's house you'll be accepted
      fully loved and understood.
   But till then my Spirit comforts as
      you walk your longest road.

Sometimes the longest road
is the one called Broken.
Never thought I'd have to walk this way.
People look then turn their faces,
tho' my deepest scars are never seen.
I see my Savior there before me.
Smiling warmly
with kindness in His eyes, He says —

Come and walk here close beside Me.
Lean on Me, I'll lead the way.
I too was broken and disfigured
then died for you My precious child.
In the Kingdom you will be restored
without blemish and made whole.
I am the risen Lamb of God and
the only scars there are My own.

Carolyn Marcusse, with a background in psychiatric nursing, wrote this poem to encourage fellow believers and challenge skeptics to explore the claims of Christ.

God's Mercy
to the
Wounded, Forsaken, and Broken

A bruised reed he will not break,

and a faintly burning wick he will not quench.

I am the Lord; I have called you in

righteousness.

I will take you by the hand and keep you.

Isaiah 42:3,6

Appendix 3

Financial Well-Being

Donald Reed, DMin
November 2023

Introduction

Before I begin, I want to thank my (nearly) lifelong friend for an invitation to provide a financial overview for those of us who are 'aging'. Don and I met in South Dakota when our children were small. We have maintained our relationship over the decades. He is a great example of stewarding/managing the resources God has given him throughout his life. I am honored to be a part of his latest literary venture.

Life is handed to us along with the responsibility of managing or stewarding the days and resources given to us. When we reach the latter stages of our life span, we likely begin to reap the benefits or liabilities of the stewardship patterns that we have practiced over our lifetimes.

We begin to experience the results of how we have treated our bodies. Healthy practices, ignoring our bodies, or even abusive practices all produce different outcomes. In later life we then become the occupants of bodies which most likely reflect years of good or harmful habits.

Other components in later life plans include family concerns, faith considerations, and other relationships that we have accumulated. Our decisions over the years usually bear fruit of what we have planted. As we sow, we shall also reap. This is certainly also true in the financial arena.

This appendix will mainly address the financial scenarios that aging people face in later years. Wise practices over a lifetime usually produce the benefit of security in later life. Unwise practices, in contrast, usually produce financial stresses that have significant impact in later years. Each scenario demands wisdom in charting a path that brings peace to us as we age.

Good Financial Planning for Self-Care

Present Financial Health Assessment

In talking about financial well-being, there are three different components to identify to gain clear understanding of one's financial health. First, there is **income**. In later years this could result from continued employment. Or it may come from retirement plan benefits accumulated in your working years. This would also include any Social Security benefits due to an individual. Or it may be the result of investments that are producing positive results in the income category. An additional income source might be from any inheritance monies received during later years. Regardless of the source, the first financial number to ascertain is one's annual income. This is fundamental to determine a sustainable standard of living for one's remaining years.

Second, there is a category known as **assets.** All savings monies would go into this category: liquid accounts such as checking and savings accounts, CDs, IRA's and other financial instruments. This would also include real assets like a home, income property, businesses, etc. Each one of these assets would be included as a possible source for one's needs in later life.

The third category is **living expenses.** This is what is spent on the basics of housing, food, transportation, insurance, travel, etc. Usually this is calculated on an annual basis for ease of comparison. If you are in the habit of using a budget, this would be easy. If you do not use a budget, it may take a little more work. You may need to reconstruct various expense categories from credit card statements, checking account records, receipts, etc. It is important for good planning to know/verify this 'outflow' of your assets to determine the financial surplus or deficit from your current lifestyle. This will likely determine your degree of financial comfort or lack thereof.

I was asked by a man who had taken my finance classes at our church to visit with his folks. They were nearing retirement age. The father had been diagnosed with Parkinson's Disease and was concerned about his need to continue working. They had gotten their finances together – their income, their expenses, their savings – before I came; and after a great conversation about their income and what they wanted to do in retirement, the outcome was obvious.

With a paid-for home, a good retirement benefit plan and living below their means all their life, they were well situated to be able to retire, go see their family members and friends and have some money for fun. With tears in their eyes, they said, "Thank You. We were so worried about this." They experienced great relief from getting their numbers in order and finding/seeing what was reality for them in their situations. We all need to either determine our financial future by the numbers or find someone to help us uncover our financial situation.

Future Planning

We can only plan for our future with good facts based on present reality. Let's look at possible scenarios and some pathways to a positive future.

Full provision

If an analysis of your financial situation reveals a sustainable future for your expected lifetime needs, congratulations! Well done. Enjoy your later years.

If, however, your financial analysis shows a shortage of income to meet annual living expenses, some needed adjustments may be necessary to relieve daily stress and worry. Let's look at a few.

Rebalancing the budget

Rebalancing the budget can be accomplished in two ways: Increase your income or reduce your expenses. Let's start with reducing expenses.

Hopefully you will have records of your spending for the recent period of time. A one-year accounting would be good as it will show both frequent and infrequent expenses. For example, regular/repeated grocery shopping versus annual/semi-annual expenses like taxes, insurance, etc. Try to reconstruct your income and spending patterns from your financial records.

When you have a copy of your expenses, you could identify which are necessary expenses and which are optional. Necessary examples would be food, transportation, housing, etc.; optional expense might be new clothing, vehicles, or expensive vacations.

If you have a spouse, conversation will be needed to identify strategies to limit your expenditures. Working on this together and reaching agreement is the pathway to peace over finances. Reach out if you need help doing this. If you are alone and/or feel overwhelmed or paralyzed by your financial situation, especially if you have any debt, you may want to seek coaching or counsel from national organizations like Christian Credit Counsellors describe more completely in (https://www.christiancreditcounselors.org) or Faith and Finance (https://www.faithfi.com/). You may also have local financial coaching organizations available. Check with your church or Senior Center for referrals.

Increasing your income

The potential for increasing your income may largely be determined by your ability and/or opportunity. First are you *able* to work, physically, emotionally, etc.? One's health and stage of life largely dictates this possibility.

Second, is there opportunity? This is especially important if you have not yet retired and can remain with your employer. Many have extended their retirement beyond the full retirement age to put themselves in a better financial position.

Here is a tip worth noting. For every year you work and contribute to Social Security beyond full retirement age, your Social Security benefits are increased by 8%, for the lifetime of your benefits. If you are pressed for income to meet your expenses, don't be tempted to take early retirement with Social Security. You could reduce your benefit by as much as 30% per check for the rest of your life. File at full retirement age, or beyond, for best benefits.

In the day in which we live (with having 'side gigs' as a normal 'extra income source'), the possibility of increased retirement income is almost unlimited. Sell things online, be a consultant, teach or tutor online courses (like English), etc. Do whatever you need to do to get to a balanced budget. You will never regret it.

Housing Challenges

Because housing for many of us is a significant cost factor, especially if we do not have a paid-for house, we need to consider some ways to reduce this significant cost factor.

Downsizing

If your housing costs devour a major portion of your income, causing stress on your budget, you may want/need to consider reducing this category of expenses. This could not only reduce monthly/annual expenses but also possibly free up equity to provide some reserve funds. Each situation will be unique. Seeking outside counsel is highly recommended. Reverse mortgages on property you own is not advised as it is usually a costly pathway. It may allow you to stay in your home longer but may also reduce your resources to a critical level. Do your research, talk to friends/acquaintances/professionals who have faced similar challenges. Financial planners, CPA's, bankers, realtors, estate planning attorneys all might be of help. Make wise decisions going forward with good information that will improve your financial situation as needed.

Family assistance

Another possible solution for reducing housing expense that is being used frequently in our day is for one's family to bring aid to their aging parents to relieve the financial stresses. Financial assistance is only one way to help. A shared living space arrangement may be available/created. If there were space to move in with a family member–son, daughter, sibling, etc.–this could be financially advantageous. Some families have provided space either with the addition of a living space for Mom/Dad or have put another unit on their property, like a tiny home, for separate living arrangement. If your family situation allows, this could be a very feasible solution. Numerous friends of ours now benefit from one of these arrangements.

Public facilities

This may also be the time to consider moving to a public facility which specializes in elder care. This may be either a small business or complexes with many residents. The more intimate elder care homes where a few people share a home with a host, individual or couple are often available. Your resources that are available will help determine what the budget allows.

Prayer

If you are a person of faith, don't overlook asking God for a solution to your financial challenges. He may bring a creative solution to your situation that will relieve your stress. It may be something totally unique that you had not imagined. He is a generous God!!

Good Financial Planning for Heir Care

Asset Management
Support for Care until Death

Good financial management will include projecting one's living expenses into the future to assure having funds available for your lifetime. A fairly simple approach to determining what one needs is to look up your expected life span, or your actuarial likelihood of years you might live. Then take your annual living expense amount and multiply this by the expected years you might live.

If you are married, you would want to consider the projected life span for each spouse. This could be affected by general health factors such as a known disease affecting one's life span. You would need to use a longer time period to calculate the reserves needed. This would be the minimum to have in place to assure your financial well-being until your death.

To plan with a bit more margin, it would be wise to extend the number of years to provide for things unknown at this point: first would be the extra medical expense in later years that could likely put demand on your assets; second, your family history of extended longevity; and thirdly, the likelihood of extended life span with the availability of good medical care. I would suggest adding another ten years of time to the equation.

Giving during lifetime – heirs/charity

For many people who have lived in a prosperous society and time, there will be a margin in the budget. This will be true both during our working years and in later years in retirement. In the secular world this is called philanthropy. In the faith world it is usually referred to as charitable giving. In either case it is practicing generosity for the benefit of others.

Whatever your context, it is recommended to give something to others in need both in your lifetime and from whatever resources you may have as you approach the end of your life. We see these opportunities in both the secular world (like the Cancer Society, United Way, etc.) and in the Christian community (churches, Christian colleges and universities, cross-cultural mission efforts, etc.)

Both religious and secular studies show that being generous, giving to others, not only results in better mental health and well-being, but also may fulfill some obligation we have to share what has been given to us. Certainly, we are all aware of a multitude of needs in our world – nearby and far away. You may recall Jesus' words, *It is more blessed to give than to receive* (Acts.

20:35). We feel better when we are generous in big and little ways. And those who benefit are blessed. Further we need to be, as one person said it, "Paying the rent for the space we take up while we are here!"

You may remember a few years ago when Warren Buffet, the investing 'Oracle of Omaha' (NE) and the richest man in the U. S., gave $36.2 billion to the Bill and Melinda Gates Foundation (Bill was the 2nd richest man in the U.S. at that time!). Some irony there!! When asked why he did that, one of his reasons was to enjoy the experience of giving while he was living. As Mark Twain said, "Do your givin' while you're livin' so you're know where it's goin'! Buffet also initiated the 'Giving Pledge' among his fellow billionaires. You can Google the details of his effort to encourage generosity – at the highest of levels of wealth. There is something good and right about being generous with whatever little or much we have.

Giving after death – heirs/charity

For many in our country who have experienced a profitable life, good health, and opportunities to acquire wealth, we will be left with what is called remainder resources. This may be in the form of liquid assets, like bank accounts and investments, or illiquid assets as in real estate, businesses etc. All of those will need attention in estate planning.

There are only three places where remainder resources can go after our death: heirs, charities, taxes (government). Good planning of asset distribution can avoid paying unnecessary taxes and leave more to share with heirs and charities. Seek good counsel on this from an accountant, financial planner or estate planning attorney. They will help with your particular situation.

The current cultural climate in the U. S. for asset distribution holds a default position of everything going to the kids! For those of us who are Jesus-followers, we would likely agree to the spiritual principle that 'God owns it all'. This is deeply rooted in Scripture, like in *(Psalm 24:1) The earth is the Lord's and everything in it* and multiple other Scriptures. There is the strong implication that the Owner (God) has some say in what is done with His possessions. We are only managers/stewards. But it is easy when thinking of our estate plans to forget to ask the Owner what He would like for us to do with our remainder resource.

This is too often true with folks who have given faithfully to their churches and missionaries yet fail to remember them in their estate plans. Some families have been creative in adopting an imaginary daughter named 'Charity' and include her in their distribution plans.

In our estate plan, if it includes excess resources for distribution after death, a place to show love to significant people and institutions that have blessed us during life is through what is called legacy giving. This could be not only for your children, if you have such, but also your church that you have loved, the missionary that you have loved and prayed for over the years, your Christian college or radio station that you love. A love gift to a charity is often easily provided through thorough estate plans.

This becomes especially germane in the western culture where most of us live, with good health care, increased longevity, opportunity for our children to prosper and enjoy excess beyond their needs. Our family is an example. We have two children in their mid-fifties. They are both in successful careers and their children are now young adults pursuing their careers. Our children are not dependent upon their folks for their well-being. This opens the door for my wife and I to include generous giving to Christian charities and other benevolent opportunities in our estate plans. We can still show love and generosity to our family members – and to other individuals and institutions that have blessed us over the years. I challenge you, whether a Jesus-follower or not, to consider leaving a legacy of generosity in your estate plan.

Laying Plans for Your Family/Heirs

Part of our responsibility as managers or stewards of whatever resources God shares with us during life is to leave plans in writing for the distribution of those assets when we are gone. If yours is a husband/wife household, upon the death of the first spouse, the assets most likely pass to the remaining spouse. However, upon the death of the second spouse, you will be doing a great favor to your heirs to leave clear instructions of your intentions for your remaining assets. This will not only make it easier for your chosen representative to carry out your wishes, but it can also avoid stressful family conflict which may have lifetime reverberations!! Highly recommended. Again, seek professional counsel – estate planning attorney, CPA, financial planner, etc.

Basic list of end-of-life documents for you to procure as needed

Will – the basic document each person/each spouse should have with clear instructions for the appointed representative. This document will be subject to state law regarding probate procedures where you reside.

This will likely incur legal expenses and delay for all but the smallest estates. To avoid probate, you will provide for all assets to be distributed through the next document – the Living Trust.

Living Trust – this document is a second place where you will leave instructions for distribution. To facilitate this pathway, you will need to, before death, move all title able property into the trust. The trust becomes the owner of your financial accounts, real estate, businesses, etc. If this is accomplished before death, you can avoid probate with its costs and delay. Highly recommended.

Health Care Directives – this document provides the name of a person who can make health care decisions for you when/if you are unable to do so.

Power of Attorney – This instruction gives power to make decisions regarding material possessions when you are no longer able or choose for someone else to act on your behalf regarding financial and property matters.

Guardianship Instructions – if you, even as a senior adult, are raising minor children, you need to have guardianship papers in place. Bless you for caring for your grandchildren. You are not alone, though it may feel like it sometimes! Over 2.5 million grandparents in the U.S. are in the same situation!!

Other documents – There are numerous other documents available to serve your special desires for handling your estate. Let me mention a couple. POD/TOD options. These acronyms stand for Payable on Death and Transfer on Death. They allow you to leave instructions with your financial institutions to, upon the verification of death, to make available the named asset to a beneficiary you have named while alive. This type of instrument takes precedence over both will and trust instructions.

End-of-life documents may be obtained online or from professional service providers like estate planning attorneys, financial planners, etc. If you are using an online service, be sure to verify that documents provided are state specific (like the Will).

Concluding Thoughts

Being good managers of our finances is our responsibility. It is particularly important as we move into our retirement years. We may be reaping the rewards of a lifetime of wise choices financially. Again, congratulations! I encourage you to *finish well*.

Or it may have, through no fault of your own (such as disaster, violence, disease, etc.), left you with sparse resources. May we all be reminded of a couple things. First, we can't take it with us when we leave. Use your time while you are here to be generous to others and richly enjoy all things God has given you *(I Tim. 6:17-19)*. Second, what we choose to do with our resources will be reflected in the life to come *(Matthew 6:19-21; I Timothy 6:17-19; Philippians 4:17)*.

Recommended Books:

God and Money – How two MBAs found True Riches at Harvard University, Baumer and Cortines
A Life God Rewards – Bruce Wilkinson, Multnomah Press

For further questions:
doreed@fellowshipnwa.org

Appendix 4

Our Bodies Replace Billions of Cells Every Day

By Mark Fischetti, Jen Christiansen

The human body replaces its own cells regularly. Scientists at the Weizmann Institute of Science in Rehovot, Israel, have finally pinned down the speed and extent of this "turnover." About a third of our body mass is fluid outside of our cells, such as plasma, plus solids, such as the calcium scaffolding of bones. The remaining two thirds is made up of roughly 30 trillion human cells.

About 72 percent of those, by mass, are fat and muscle, which last an average of 12 to 50 years, respectively. But we have far more, tiny cells in our blood, which live only three to 120 days, and lining our gut, which typically live less than a week. Those two groups, therefore, make up much of the turnover. About 330 billion cells are replaced daily, equivalent to about 1 percent of all our cells. In 80 to 100 days, 30 trillion will have replenished—*the equivalent of a new you.*

This article was originally published with the title "A New You in 80 Days" in Scientific American 324, 4, 76 (April 2021)

. . . For I am fearfully and wonderfully made. (From Psalm 139:13–16, Author's emphasis)

The sun shall be no more
your light by day,
nor for brightness shall the moon
give you light;[2]
but the Lord will be your everlasting light,
and your God will be your glory.
Your sun shall no more go down,
nor your moon withdraw itself;
for the Lord will be your everlasting light,
and your days of mourning shall be ended.

Isaiah 60:19–20

End Notes

For Those Who Need More Information

Chapter 1 Accepting

1. **Page 17. The Importance of Staying Hydrated** Constance Schein, RN. Heathy Aging. *http://www.aegisliving.com/resources-center/the-importance-of-staying-hydrated/* (February 28, 2020).

2. **Page 17. Botox Injections: Purpose, Procedure, Risks, Results.** Arefa Cssoobhopy, MD. MDH. WebMD *https://www.webmd.com/beauty/cosmetic-procedures-botox* (July 24, 2020).

3. **Page 19. Why it is Harder to Stand Up as You Age** Nish Manek, MD. BBC Science-Focus Magazine. *http://www.sciencefocus.com/the-human-body/why-its-harder-to-stand-up-as-tou-get-older* (July 1, 2023).

4. **Page 21. Suicide and Older Adults: What You Should know. National Council on Aging.** National Council on Aging. *http://www.ncoa.org/article/suicide-and-older-adults-what-you-should-know* (December 8, 2023).

Chapter 3 Suffering

5. Page 50. *Live Younger Longer*, Stephen Kopecky, M.D. Mayo Foundation for Medical Education and Research (MFMER). Mayo Clinic Press (2021), Rochester MN pp223

6. Page 54. Elisabeth Elliot
http://www.azquotes.com/quote424412

Chapter 4 Change

7. Page 84. Television Set (History)
https://en.wikipedia.org/wiki/Television_set

Chapter 6 Wisdom

8. Page 121. James M Barrie (1860–1937)
https://www.brainyquote.com/quotes/james_m_barrie_106441 .

Chapter 7 Relationships

9. Page 129. Intuits tribal custom of taking care of their elderly
https://en.wikipedia.org/wiki/Senicide

10. Page 133. My Mom's advice . . . , *Laura Hook (1913-1991), Mother of Jan Brauer, editor*

Chapter 8 The Autumn of Life

11. Page 146. Autumn Meaning in Life . . . Tina Swain, MA, 3 Lessons from the Fall . . . *https://www.linkedin.com/in/tinaaswain?trk=article-ssr-frontend-pulse_publisher-author-card* (October 31, 2023)

12. Page 153. Swain. op. cit.

13. **Page 160.** Mark Buchanan, God Walk: Moving at the Speed of your Soul, (Grand Rapids, Mich.: Zondervan, 2020), 87, 92.

14. **Page 165.** Sarah Young, Jesus Calling app, Be Prepared to Suffer for Me (October 14)

Chapter 9 Aging

15. **Page 176.** Morning Star, Vol. 40 No.11. Radium, MN. (October 31, 2023).

Tell of All His Wondrous Works

Oh give thanks to the LORD;

call upon his name;

make known his deeds among the peoples!

Sing to him, sing praises to him;

tell of all his wondrous works!

Glory in his holy name;

let the hearts of those who seek the LORD

rejoice!

Seek the LORD and his strength.

seek his presence continually!

Psalm 105:1–4

A Word of Thanks
Acknowledgments

Writing a book is not a solitary effort. Although the burden of such an effort falls to the author—a job of writing, rewriting, and rewriting—others helped give birth to the book to see the light of day. Because of their commitment to do what they do best, they made it possible for others to read what is written to be a pleasant experience.

It is to these folks that I want to give a special word of thanks and deep appreciation for their excellent and self-sacrificing labor of love.

During the formation of the *Gift of Aging*, the **Sojourners** adult Sunday school class at Colonial Presbyterian Church, Kansas City, MO provided many words of senior wisdom that are woven within its pages. Deeply appreciated! Thank you all.

My technical editor, **Jan Brauer,** was my gaffe (not giraffe) hunter. She tenaciously tracked down my grammatical and spelling errors. And freely challenged my words when they went astray. She added her endorsement on the back cover as she did for my previous books. Thanks, Jan.

If Jan checked the recipe, my content editor, **Paula Freeman,** put the icing on the cake. Her effort resulted in a generous supply of red ink that made the finished product attractive and delightfully readable. She graciously contributed her skill and experience by writing, *A Season for Becoming Yourself.* Page 158. A wonderful job! Thanks. **Paula** is also the author of two books, *Learning to Be Me Without You–A Story of Love, Loss, and Coming Home (Redemption Press, Enumclaw, WA. 2022)*, and *A Place I Didn't Belong–Hope for Adoptive Moms. (Carpenter's Son Publishing, Franklin, TN. 2013).*

As always, the result of editing by others is always a productive lesson in humility for the author.

Without question, the artistic rendering of the book's cover is exceptional. As she has done with my most recent books, **Lili Zoller**, my daughter-in-law, provides her suburb graphic talent to create an eye-catching design for *The Gift of Aging.* The author has only a few seconds to invite the curious eye of a potential reader to pick up the book and begin their journey through its pages. **Lili** has skillfully helped capture the reader's curiosity. A special thanks to her.

Patsy Klontz, friend, and fellow lover of words did the necessary final proof-read of *The Gift of Aging* before the book hit the streets. Thank you so much.

A special friend, author, and my mentor, **Charlotte Adelsperger.**, has been my cheer leader for *The Gift of*

Aging in addition to other books I've written over the years. Thank you for your counsel and encouragement.

A word of thanks to my publisher, **BookBaby**, Pennsauken, New Jersey, who has professionally shepherded this and two previous books through the publication process to marketing.

* * * *

With deep gratitude to my project team, my primary thanks belong to the **Lord Jesus Christ**. Each time I sat at my computer to write, I prayed, "Lord this is your book. I don't know what to say. Please fill my mind with your thoughts. Allow me to experience your presence as You guide my fingers to tap the keys. May my wandering eyes keep their focus on You. My desire is for your glory. Also, graciously bless and encourage every reader of this book." If there is any praise or appreciation expressed after you read this book, please be sure you say, "Thank you" to the one who made this book possible—*Jesus Christ*.

Doxology

Now to him who is able

to keep you from stumbling and

to present you blameless

before the presence of his glory with great joy,

to the only God, our Savior,

through Jesus Christ our Lord,

be glory, majesty, dominion, and authority,

before all time and now and forever. Amen.

Jude 24–25

Other Books by Donald Zoller

Grow Strong in Today's World

The Master Weaver*

Living Life in The 4th Quarter

This Ugly Disease

The Last Shofar

Learning To Suffer God's Way

Except as noted, these books are available
through online book retailers

*Available only through the publisher's Bookshop
https://store.bookbaby.com

Additional copies of *The Gift of Aging* are available
at most online book retailers.

Including the Publisher's Bookshop
https://store.bookbaby.com

About the Author

Donald Zoller is the author of seven books, including *The Gift of Aging*. In addition to his books, he has written several articles, essays, and tutorials. Before becoming an active writer, Don served as a professional cartographer for forty years with the Federal government. Over the years, he invested much of his free time as a volunteer in domestic and international mission ministries. Don graduated from the University of Sioux Falls, South Dakota. He now savors with satisfaction the eighty-eight years of life God has given him. His wife, Beverley went home to be with her Lord in 2016. Don has three sons, two daughters-in-law, and two grandchildren. He currently lives in Leawood, Kansas. *(2024)*

www.truthinscripture.net

dhzoller@outlook.com